—For Grace Anne

—And to our clients and students who know loss intimately
and still demonstrate the courage to suffer.
You have taught us deep strength, and we have learned
what flourishing is because of you.

Contents

THE COURAGE TO SUFFER

1 ⚘

An Existential Positive Psychology Framework

"But there was no need to be ashamed of tears,
for tears bore witness that a man had the greatest
of courage, the courage to suffer."
—VIKTOR E. FRANKL, *Man's Search for Meaning*

OUR LIVES have been profoundly shaped by suffering.

In early 2010, we were beginning to build our careers and felt the promise of a somewhat expected future. Sara, while completing her supervision hours toward her clinical license, was working with families of children with chronic and significant medical needs. Daryl was completing his fourth year of doctoral work and was in the thick of dissertation research studying how people find meaning in life, with hopes of going on the academic job market in the fall. We were feeling settled, so we started trying to get pregnant. And like most people, we didn't notice that life was going as planned.

Four months later, everything changed.

In April, we received a phone call that upended our world and irrevocably altered our lives. Daryl's brother Tim underwent surgery that did not go as expected. We immediately flew to Colorado to be with family. Within a few short weeks, Tim died at age thirty-four, leaving his wife to raise their three young children under the age of six. Because of the genetic nature of Tim's illness, there was a high likelihood that we would experience a similar fate as Tim and his wife. We were haunted by the existential question: Would Daryl develop the same condition that took Tim's life? To compound our grief, one specialist stated that, given the genetic nature of Tim's condition, we should not have children. It was one loss after another.

Years after this devastating blow to our dreams and our identity, we began to seek consultation and additional specialists' opinions, who eventually gave us the green light to start a family. Our lost dream was given new hope. However, after almost two years of trying, we were told, with a sense of finality, that we would not be parents. Our infertility diagnosis further added to our grief, and our suffering was palpable. This pain and those experiences had become *part of us* and in many ways *shaped us*; how could we remove the pain or forget our experiences? We sought the help of friends and professionals, but the reality was we could not be unbroken. This was now our story.

The Need for a New Approach to Suffering

As a professionally trained psychologist and clinical social worker, respectively, we challenged every cognitive distortion that we had: "our life was over" (catastrophizing), "this is all our fault" (personalizing), "we're inadequate" (emotional reasoning), and we were still left with the simple fact that we would not be parents and that Daryl's genetic future was unknown. However, our story was not a cognitive distortion; our suffering was not a set of irrational thoughts that needed to be corrected. No amount of therapeutic mental gymnastics could make us feel unbroken. We needed a new approach—a completely different way to think about suffering that allowed us to hold the pain in authentic ways while desperately seeking to flourish.

Clinical work has long focused on alleviating suffering. However, not every therapeutic model is designed to help those in persistent, recurring, or unsolvable suffering. Many perspectives approach mental health concerns as discrete negative events that can be directly resolved through cognitive adaptation, emotion regulation, or behavioral modification strategies. Boiled down to its most basic level, many clinical approaches view suffering as a *problem to be fixed*, and then, once the symptoms subside, disregard the effect of the event itself. This strategy falls short, however, when the event and its effects have fundamentally changed the individual's life and cannot be resolved. There is no fixing death, infertility, loss of a dream, or the permanent shift of one's identity. Instead, these approaches must account for deeply painful situations that alter your client's life in ways that cannot be reversed or solved. Our framework is designed precisely for such situations. Put succinctly, we posit that *suffering is an inherent part of life that must be engaged*. And we suggest that your clinical approach should embody that truth.

OVERVIEW OF FRAMEWORK

We propose an existential positive psychology approach to suffering. It highlights the necessity of identifying the core concerns underlying each person's experience, as well as the importance of building strong relationships, values, and virtues as ways to promote flourishing in the midst of suffering. It is unique from other clinical approaches in that the centerpiece of this model is cultivating meaning, a component shared by both existential and positive psychology perspectives. Synthesizing these frameworks can provide a rich approach to engage your clients in their darkest and most difficult times of life, by honoring their pain *and* finding ways to experience a rich and full life during that pain.

Existential approaches to psychotherapy, popularized by individuals such as Viktor Frankl and Irvin Yalom, contend that anxiety and suffering arise, in part, from the persistent isolation of all humans and the inherent meaninglessness of the world, where the only certainty is death.[1,2] Each person is inherently alone and is wired to find ways to connect with others and create meaning while they are alive.

Part of the existential process is accepting, and coming to terms with, these givens of human existence. Our approach provides a pathway for exploring the depth of your client's situation by examining what central fears are uncovered by their suffering and how it may be affecting their ability to flourish. As people identify core features of human existence as root causes of their suffering, they can learn to create meaning *from within*, rather than expecting to find meaning from the outside—regardless of their circumstances.

Meaning is also a central feature of the positive psychology movement, which developed as a response to the majority of psychological research and clinical work that had focused solely on viewing people through the lens of mental disorders and abnormal functioning.[3] Psychology had become narrowly focused on the negative: distress, dysfunction, disorders, and disease. But this focus on the negative provides an incomplete view of human nature. Positive psychology addresses that "other half" by emphasizing how character strengths, virtues, and meaning contribute to the good life. In short, whereas most other psychological perspectives help people cope with mental illness, positive psychology helps people cultivate full and flourishing lives.

The synergistic blend of the existential psychology perspective and the positive psychology perspective creates a shared goal: *building meaning in all circumstances*. Drawing from existential and positive psychology,[4] our approach examines the deep, underlying existential concerns that suffering exposes, while focusing on building meaning and promoting a full, whole life that is marked by authenticity and concern for others. This approach requires balancing both motivations of depth and growth: Without sufficient depth, your clients will not fully address the core root of their suffering; and without sufficient growth, your clients may stagnate and become overwhelmed by feelings of hopelessness, depression, and despair. Your role as therapist is to help your clients engage both motivations by helping them cultivate meaning. This intersection of perspectives is depicted in Figure 1.

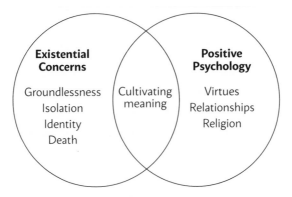

FIGURE 1. The existential positive psychology framework.

DEFINING TERMS: SUFFERING, MEANING, AND HOW THE TWO RELATE

Before we describe how to work with your clients in the process of suffering, it is important to define suffering and meaning, and clarify how to approach the relationship between the two concepts.

The Difference between Pain and Suffering

Pain exists when your client is experiencing an event or a pattern of thinking that (a) is explainable (i.e., has a clear source or reason), (b) has a relatively distinct trajectory (i.e., appears to be resolvable given enough time), and (c) is relatively focused (i.e., affects one primary area of life); in such cases, your typical therapeutic approaches may be sufficient. Consider a client who seeks support after the expected death of an elderly parent. Most therapeutic approaches, such as cognitive-behavioral therapy (CBT), are well-suited to help a client alter their thoughts about a parent's death, help them process their grief, encourage them to explore and express their emotions, and begin to navigate relational changes in their family. In situations like these, the client's pain has an easily identifiable source and can be addressed by your usual treatment modalities.

However, other forms of emotional pain are qualitatively different. Whereas pain may have some form of a solution, suffering is persistent and may not be resolvable. Some suffering is so profound, so violating, or so dogged, that it fundamentally changes people in indelible ways and forces them to come to terms with core existential realities of life. Situations like these are *unexplainable or violating, persistent and enduring,* and *fundamentally life-changing.* You can experience pain without suffering, but you cannot experience suffering without pain. Our approach is designed to help you work with clients who are suffering.

Consider a client who seeks support after the expected death of a parent from amyotrophic lateral sclerosis (ALS), a genetic and heritable disease that also has implications that affect not only your client but the immediate family as well. The death of their parent elicits existential concerns about their own death and the lives of their children. You could attempt to employ a CBT approach and help the client reframe how they think about dying or help them cope with the emotional distress of losing a parent, but you would be working from a limited perspective that only addresses a resolution from the aspect of losing a parent. What do you do with the very real idea that your client's own health is at risk and that they will have to live with that uncertainty? Our approach acknowledges that the pain your client feels is valuable and must be wrestled with and integrated, not removed. Instead, your client can learn to bear this pain.

What Is Meaning?

Building meaning is the key to helping your clients who are suffering. We define *meaning as the subjective feeling that my experiences and life make sense, matter, and are purposeful.*[5] Researchers agree that there are three main components of meaning: coherence, significance, and purpose.[6] A sense of *coherence* arises when people can make sense of events—when their experiences fit into their worldview or set of beliefs. People usually feel coherence when they explain why things happened in a way that is consistent with how they see the world. The central question pertaining to coherence is: *Does this make sense?*

People experience *significance* when they feel like they have worth, value, and that they matter or feel connected to something larger than themselves. People usually feel significant when they have reciprocal relationships, when their work is consequential, and when they are making a positive, lasting contribution to the world. The central question pertaining to significance is: *Do I matter?*

People achieve a sense of *purpose* when they have broader intentions toward which they can place their energy and effort. A sense of purpose gives people a reason for their actions and helps frame your client's sense of identity. The central question pertaining to purpose is: *Why am I here?*

Each facet of meaning acts as a protective factor during times of suffering. Coherence *translates* events in ways that make sense; significance helps people *transcend* themselves and connect with others; and purpose *transforms* experiences, including pain and suffering, into something greater.

Meaning and Happiness Are Not the Same

People may use the terms "meaning" and "happiness" interchangeably, but it's important to distinguish the difference between the two concepts. As an example, parents often report less marital satisfaction after having children compared to nonparents.[7] In addition, the more children a couple has, the less satisfied they are in their relationship. Cross-cultural research confirms these results and also shows that Americans experience the strongest negative effects.[8] Yet most of these parents would likely report that having a child is incredibly meaningful and significant; the meaning, not necessarily happiness, derived from parenting is what contributes to parental well-being.[9] Despite its strain on happiness, many do not forgo being parents in order to be happier. They choose meaning.

Another study directly compared happiness and meaning to clarify how they differ. People report being happy when stress, struggles, and negative events are largely absent. Meaning, in contrast, was present when people reported being stressed, struggling, or were experiencing adversity.[10] Whereas hardships are at odds with happiness, people find meaning in such circumstances.

To compare meaning and happiness over time, a longitudinal study followed seventy-nine people who were completing a practicum course in a mental health setting at the beginning of the study. They completed weekly journals while enrolled in their practicum course and then later filled out surveys on their coping, emotional regulation, grit, gratitude, and well-being. The results revealed that meaning-making was strongly and positively related to adapting well to future negative events. Happiness, on the other hand, did not predict adaptive functioning in the future.[11] Cultivating meaning *now* can better prepare people for adversity or suffering again in the *future*. This research provides powerful evidence that meaning, rather than happiness, is an important component in a flourishing life.

Why We Are Focusing on Meaning

As previously noted, meaning-focused therapy is integral to positive client outcomes. For example, a meta-analysis of sixty clinical trials with more than 3,700 people indicated that meaning-focused approaches significantly improved clients' quality of life and decreased psychological stress relative to treatment-as-usual.[12] The benefits in reducing psychological stress occurred because clients were able to increase their sense of meaning via therapeutic interventions.

But do meaning-focused approaches work with clients who are suffering and facing existential concerns? Research from work with patients who have cancer suggests that they do. A clinical intervention with more than 250 late-stage patients who have cancer revealed that those who received meaning-centered group psychotherapy over the course of eight weeks reported better outcomes than those who received the standard treatment on a host of psychologically relevant variables: They were less depressed, more hopeful, and reported less physical distress, greater spiritual well-being, and higher quality of life.[13] Although standard treatment is helpful, the improvements were significantly greater for the meaning-focused group, especially on indicators of severe despair (e.g., wishing for a hastened death, hopelessness), leading the researchers to assert that meaning-focused approaches that address existential issues are more effective in these cases than traditional interventions.

Another large-scale study of cancer survivors, based on more than 8,400 cancer survivors from the American Cancer Society's Study of Cancer Survivors-II database, revealed that religious and spiritual beliefs were associated with better mental and physical functioning, precisely because they provided individuals with a strong sense of meaning in life.[14] Put differently, meaning was the mechanism by which beliefs led to flourishing. This research provides direct evidence that cultivating meaning amid suffering, especially in the wake of events that do not seem to have a readily apparent or available resolution, is particularly beneficial for clients.

However, there's an important caveat in this research. A systematic review of seventy different research studies highlighted that the positive health benefits of meaning seem to be reserved for those who find meaning, not simply those who search for it.[15] It is important to keep in mind that helping your client *find* a sense of meaning is crucial, because meaning may be the biggest protective factor when life brings suffering.

The key to working with your clients—especially if their suffering may lead them to feel as though they will never get through it—is *building meaning in life*.

The Role of Meaning in Suffering

We want to clarify three points about the role of meaning in suffering. First, we are not suggesting that pain is justified through meaning. Finding meaning can help transform already deeply painful experiences into something more without invalidating or excusing them. Second, we also are not suggesting that people intentionally seek out pain in their lives as a pathway to flourishing. Although meaning can help transform pain en route to a flourishing life, other avenues toward flourishing are likely available. Rather, we are suggesting that when people are suffering, cultivating meaning helps transform such experiences into something greater than the pain, making the pain more bearable. Third, without denying or invalidating their pain, you can help your client see that (a) they still matter, greatly; (b) they can broaden their perspective and connect with others, a larger cause, or the Divine; and (c) the experience of pain does not preclude them from contributing meaningfully to the lives of others. In their suffering, the translational, transcendent, and transformative features of meaning may not alleviate all their pain, but they may certainly help widen their perspective when the pain feels overwhelming. Thus, the paradox of suffering is this: *Suffering makes it challenging to find meaning but meaning is precisely what is needed to flourish.*

THE ARC OF SUFFERING: PHASES OF DARKNESS

Suffering is deeply personal, and no two people experience it the same way. However, clinical experience and psychological research suggest a typical pattern of how suffering unfolds over time in the lives of your clients. We suggest that thinking about the process of suffering is like moving through different *phases of darkness*.

- **Sunset** is the initial phase when suffering strikes and your clients are likely feeling disoriented and isolated. Your primary tasks will be to *assess* your client's initial sense of meaning (and from where meaning is found) and help them to *stabilize*. By understanding what gives their life meaning, through understanding their cultural worldviews, you can engage them with humility and start to lay a foundation for future therapeutic work.

- **Dusk** requires helping to push your clients into the darkness of their pain. This will bring about the goal of *acceptance*. Without acceptance, your client will be unable to flourish in their suffering. This often requires the client to overcome natural tendencies to avoid pain and can be helped by implementing various techniques designed to build the client's capacity to withstand the discomfort of pressing into existentially unsettling concerns.

- **Midnight** can be the most challenging part of the suffering process, as it requires clients to question and deconstruct their beliefs. Most clinical approaches end before this phase, as suffering is understood to be a discrete issue to be accepted, whereas the emotional and behavioral effects are disturbances to be mitigated. However, a full and complete engagement of suffering often requires your client to question, doubt, or deconstruct many of their deeply held beliefs that have been shattered by suffering through the process of *active questioning*.

- **Dawn** is a period of reconstruction, where your clients can practice the _autonomy_ of rebuilding their beliefs in ways that are authentic to their experiences of suffering. This allows clients to retell their stories of suffering in a way that honors their pain and allows the space for them to revise their identity to be congruent with how their experience has indelibly changed their life.

- **Daylight** is the phase in which your clients can begin to live _authentically_, choosing a life that fits with their revised beliefs and identity, learning to balance their desire for meaning, and anticipating how to adaptively cope with future suffering. By building existential resilience, your clients will be better equipped to encounter the consistent reminders of their suffering and tackle future struggles as they arise.

Figure 2 presents an overview of our model.

bargaining - denial — acceptance - meaning

| **Sunset** | **Dusk** | **Midnight** | **Dawn** | **Daylight** |
| Sting of Suffering | Into the Darkness | Deconstruction | Reconstruction | Living Authentically |

FIGURE 2. The phases of darkness.

Although this progression looks linear and formulaic, three clarifications are needed. First, suffering looks different for each person, and the application of this framework requires your own clinical insight. Second, we acknowledge that we have been afforded privileges that many of your clients may have not; our education, socioeconomic status, and vocational opportunities have all likely been protective factors that helped us. Although suffering affects each of us, it might fall more harshly on the marginalized. We provide several guiding principles that can help frame your work with your clients, and we will also provide various case examples. It is important to use your own discretion to best determine where these examples fit and where they do not. Third, and related to this, not every person moves through the phases of darkness in this order. Your clients may skip around phases, go back to previous phases, or be in any one of the phases when they first meet with you. Use your wisdom to determine how to best support your clients, and resist trying to fit them into a "one-size-fits-all" mold of suffering. Life is messier than that, and suffering is wildly unpredictable. To help you put this framework into practice, we offer several principles that guide our approach.

GUIDING PRINCIPLES

When using this approach, these principles should permeate your work with clients across all phases of darkness.

- **Pain is not bad.** It is not bad to experience pain—it is just painful. Although the feeling of pain is aversive, it is a natural part of life and a near certainty when coping with some of life's most difficult moments. Your clients can choose (to some degree) how to view pain and their relationship to it. And in some cases, the pain is a necessary part of growth. Pain is information. It can help us understand more clearly. This does not mean that people should invite unnecessary pain, nor does it mean that you should try to highlight how someone's pain is "good." However, your clients may be able to experience growth after identifying and naming their pain. Running from or failing to acknowledge pain can make things worse.
- **Suffering is an existential issue.** When your clients' worldview is rendered inadequate to explain the pain and suffering in their life, they will face existential questions of uncertainty, isolation, identity, and death. Without a suitable set of beliefs that can endure this tension, they experience heightened existential

anxiety, which further perpetuates their distress. Addressing existential concerns is a central part of helping your clients break the cyclical nature of suffering. They must wrestle with these concerns and find a suitable approach that will help restore a sense of existential security. For some, it requires reassembling or revising their worldview; for others, it means living in the tension of doubt and uncertainty.

- **Suffering and flourishing are not mutually exclusive.** Your clients do not have to wait for suffering to subside in order to flourish, as suffering may persist. Flourishing does not always lead to happiness, yet it is possible to live a rich and meaningful life in the midst of pain and struggle. In many cases, people can transform their pain into something greater than themselves. Most clients can find meaning and thrive in their current circumstances, even when their struggles persist.
- **Cultivating meaning is the key to flourishing in suffering.** By cultivating meaning, people can experience a full and flourishing life, despite their circumstances. It helps people translate events into a coherent narrative, transcend themselves to connect with other people and with God or the sacred, and transform experiences by broadening perspectives. It is how they transform their pain. Part of your role will be to work with your clients to find and build meaning in both the joyful and painful parts of their lives.
- **Flourishing in suffering is a continual process.** Because the events that led to suffering were complex and unfolded slowly over time—or were major life events that drastically shifted how your clients see the world—they cannot be quickly dispatched or solved. Facing deep-seeded existential questions takes time. Viewing flourishing in suffering as an ongoing process can also relieve undue pressure to find a quick and simple answer.

It allows space for your clients to live with the tension of their beliefs, many of which continue to change and evolve.

These principles can help orient you to work with your clients as they move through the phases of darkness. Your work together will require courage—from *you* to sit in the presence of your clients' pain and ask difficult questions that name the source of their suffering, and from *your clients* to engage with and accept their pain rather than avoid, dismiss, or minimize it. As Viktor Frankl's opening quote poignantly points out, their tears, and (we would add) your presence, will attest to the human capacity not only to endure suffering but also the bravery to flourish in the midst of it.

"In what ways has your suffering influenced your world view?"

2 ❊

Existential Themes of Suffering

"I have learned things in the dark that I could never have
learned in the light, things that have saved my life over and
over again, so that there is really only one logical conclusion.
I need darkness as much as I need light."

—BARBARA BROWN TAYLOR, *Learning to Walk in the Dark*

AN ENCOUNTER with the darkness is disorienting and reveals vulnerability. As your clients move through the dark seasons of their
suffering, they often feel fearful and exposed. Behind this fear lie
certain deep and pressing existential concerns that undermine their
sense of meaning. For genuine and lasting flourishing to occur, it is
important to rebuild meaning by addressing the existential threats
that compound your clients' pain.

Previous work from existential psychotherapy has identified four
core concerns that underlie people's mental health struggles (because
they undermine feelings of meaning): groundlessness, isolation,
identity, and death.[16,17] These concerns are central themes in how
people experience suffering and can erode people's sense of meaning in life. When clients experience groundlessness, they struggle to
find coherence, eliciting questions of whether they can make sense
of their suffering. Feelings of isolation can undermine perceptions of
significance, causing clients to wonder if they matter. Wrestling with
identity can cast doubt on one's sense of purpose, leading them to ask
why they are here. Death pressures all these dimensions of meaning

and can cause clients to wonder if there is really any meaning to be found in life at all. Figure 3 summarizes how these themes are related to meaning, and which questions arise in your work with clients.

EXISTENTIAL THEME	RELEVANT ASPECT OF MEANING	PRESSING QUESTION
Groundlessness	Coherence	Does this make sense?
Isolation	Significance	Do I matter? S.N.
Identity	Purpose	Why am I here? S.N.
Death	All	Is life meaningful at all?

FIGURE 3. The relationship between existential themes of suffering, relevant dimensions of meaning, and pressing questions that need to be addressed.

When you've identified that your client is persistently suffering, your responsibility is to decipher the client's presenting concerns and how they may fall into one of the four broader categories of existential themes. Doing so will help your client identify the root fears and anxieties that may be keeping them mired in suffering. It will also help you better understand which dimension of meaning may be the most affected, and where you can start working to cultivate meaning.

EXISTENTIAL THEMES OF SUFFERING

Groundlessness: The Loss of Control and the Burden of Freedom

IMPORTANCE. A perceived sense of control is an important part of healthy psychological functioning,[18] as it leads to feelings of safety and effectiveness and allows your clients to make plans and expect their actions to bring about desired outcomes. However, when people experience groundlessness—or a loss of control—they feel helpless, as if the world is acting upon them instead. On the other end of the spectrum, being overwhelmed with seemingly endless possible future outcomes (i.e., too much freedom) can feel paralyzing.

SYMPTOMS/EXPRESSIONS. Your clients may report feeling general anxiety, panic attacks, or specific anxiety regarding the lack of control in one, or several, areas of their life. They may report posttraumatic stress disorder (PTSD)-like symptoms (e.g., avoidance, inability to experience pleasurable emotions, distorted beliefs about the world) or obsessive compulsive-like symptoms (e.g., obsessive and recurrent thoughts about losing control of health or relationships, or compulsive behavior to try to regain control) as an attempt to create illusionary control. Moreover, this feeling of groundlessness can give way to depression and hopelessness. Your clients might wonder, *"If life is largely outside of my control and unpredictable, how do I make sense of the world?"* Groundlessness challenges views of coherence.

Isolation: Being Alone

IMPORTANCE. Given that part of the human condition is a strong motivation for interpersonal relationships (although there are interpersonal differences in how many or how deep relationships people seek), when your clients experience isolation, it runs counter to the conditions necessary to thrive. A long line of research reveals that social exclusion—being left out, rejected, ostracized, excluded from a group, or otherwise alone—is associated with myriad negative mental health symptoms, such as depression and meaninglessness.[19] It can also cause people to act aggressively, which may further isolate them when they lash out at those people in their lives who care deeply about them.[20]

xavier

SYMPTOMS/EXPRESSIONS. Concerns about isolation have profound effects on your clients' daily life and interpersonal functioning. This may come out in two primary ways. First, it may make maintaining their current relationships more difficult. Your clients may report increased anxiety during social situations or difficulty engaging in or maintaining relationships. Clients may begin to act defensively or "put up walls" in their current relationships, preemptively withdrawing emotionally, physically, or psychologically as a way of protecting themselves from future loss. Your clients may also report depression and a lack of motivation to seek out relationships.

Your clients may also quickly form superficial relationships or fail to hold proper boundaries in the relationships they currently have. They may fixate on how their relationships will unfold in the future, wondering if their relationships will persist in the future, who they can count on during times of need, and whether current relationships will also end in abandonment. In short, the fear of isolation may lead to anxiety, depression, and relational discord and dissatisfaction. Your clients may ask, "*Does anyone love me? Am I a person of worth? Do I matter?*" Isolation undermines people's feelings of significance.

Identity: Determining Who I Am

IMPORTANCE. As clients wrestle with the narrative of how their suffering fits into the story of their lives, they may encounter challenges of identity. Developmentally, researchers suggest that early adulthood is a prime time for people to try to establish their identity, so be aware if this concern is present when working with young adults.[21] However, identity-related questions can arise throughout life, often during periods of stress or transition, such as among new parents or empty-nesters. Perhaps just as readily as people begin to wrestle with the question of *who am I*, they quickly turn to questions of purpose: *Why am I here?* Part of developing a narrative view of oneself and coming to terms with one's identity is cultivating a clear sense of how to contribute to the world. Your clients' struggle around identity may evoke certain questions: *"What is my purpose in this life? How can I make a difference?"* Identity and purpose go hand-in-hand.

SYMPTOMS/EXPRESSIONS. Because a person's identity serves as a consistent and central organizing theme in life, issues surrounding identity may have some of the widest-spread effects on their mental health and behavior, both outwardly and inwardly. Outwardly, the biggest effects may be on your clients' relationships. Relationally, your clients may struggle with knowing where to fit in and how to relate with people, especially if they are coming to terms with a newfound identity. Inwardly, your clients are experiencing a major adjustment to a new normal: a reality that they did not invite nor necessarily want.

Identity shifts, such as the loss of dreams or expectations, should not be taken lightly. Your clients may have organized their entire life around a particular goal or dream that is now unattainable. Their loss is real, and the accompanying grief can be fierce and powerful. Moreover, they might experience uncertainty and anxiety as they try to navigate how to survive, let alone thrive, in this new set of circumstances. There is no playbook for how to raise three children on your own as a widow or how to cope with the reality that you have been given a finite time to live. Your clients may report significant stress, disrupted sleep, physical health problems, and a host of mental health concerns. They may begin questioning how the ways they view themselves and the world, and what they consider to be divine or sacred (e.g., God), fit into implicit or explicit beliefs. This critical examination, and the potential unravelling of such beliefs, may cause anxiety and uncertainty.

Death: Loss (of Life)

IMPORTANCE. Reminders of death—surviving a near-death experience, receiving a medical diagnosis, the death of a loved one, or broader scale reminders like acts of terrorism, the threat of nuclear war, or the loss of life on a global scale—push death into the foreground of our attention. Worldviews act as buffers for anxiety elicited by reminders of death by providing a clear and organized way of understanding the world.[22] For many people, religious beliefs constitute the bulk of their worldview, especially when it pertains to death. These beliefs help them cope with the reality of death by providing answers regarding the nature of this life (e.g., God will protect me) and how to conquer death (e.g., there is an afterlife). Situations that make death a primary concern begin to put pressure on cultural worldviews, exposing any flaws in logic or potential contradictions. Your clients might notice such tensions, asking, *"How do I make sense of life when I know it is going to end? If everyone dies and is eventually forgotten, do I really matter? What's the point of life if we all die anyway?"* In turn, death pressures all your clients' assumptions about meaning, leading them to ultimately ask, *"Is there any meaning to be found in this life at all?"*

Death is so strongly related to suffering because the end of life is particularly problematic for people's sense of meaning. For some, death may motivate them to live authentically and fully embrace the limited number of days they have.[23] For others, this reminder undercuts their motivation and sinks them into a deep sense of meaninglessness, where they question whether their efforts to build meaning are even worth the trouble.

SYMPTOMS/EXPRESSIONS. When confronted with death, three responses are common: (a) denial/suppression, (b) anxiety/preoccupation, and (c) hopelessness/depression. Some people may deny or suppress thinking about death by staying busy or numbing their emotions (e.g., through substances, Netflix binging, excessive Internet use, or throwing themselves into their career). Other clients may report considerable anxiety. Some become preoccupied with concerns that they, or other people, will die soon. They may be vigilantly focused on activities to protect themselves and others (e.g., concerned about their own or their loved one's diet, exercise, and safety), and some of these concerns or activities may reach unhealthy levels that impair daily functioning. They may also begin to wrestle with, and have anxiety regarding, their religious and spiritual beliefs. Finally, some clients may report hopelessness and depression. They may feel overwhelmed by the reality of death and its inescapability, and they may question what the point of life is, if everyone is just destined to die (and be forgotten). They may show lack of motivation, begin to withdraw from relationships, and perform poorly at work. They may give up doing things that once brought them pleasure. They may change their worldview to be more nihilistic, embracing a view of the world that is cold, uncaring, and ultimately meaningless. The effects of concerns surrounding death are considerable and powerful—and a part of life.

CASE EXAMPLES

Not all your clients will easily identify, and speak in terms of, these existential themes of suffering. For example, not every client says, "I'm feeling isolated," or "I'm experiencing a lack of control." Therefore, we provide three case examples that highlight some of these different existential concerns, including how these themes tend to lurk beneath more manifest symptoms and how they keep people stuck in suffering. We will be drawing on these examples throughout the book. It is important to mention that although these case examples are rooted in Sara's clinical work, identifying information and key details have been changed to protect the clients' anonymity and maintain confidentiality.

Joanna

Joanna is a first-time parent in her early 40s who has made an appointment to discuss feelings of depression and anger. Joanna had been a high-ranking business executive for a global company and placed most of her identity in her career and hard-earned achievements. She decided her next goal would be to raise a child on her own since she had not found a suitable partner. She had everything planned: the nursery, childcare, and her maternity leave. When she was twenty-eight weeks pregnant, she became eclamptic and started seizing due to high blood pressure. Ultimately, she experienced brain hemorrhaging and was rushed in for an emergency C-section. As a result of her medical complications, she permanently lost sight in one eye, was unable to maintain balance as she walked, and had severe weakness in her dominant hand and foot. Her son was born premature and was developmentally delayed and medically complex. Joanna found it difficult and painful to imagine the reality of her life as it was. She was unable to maintain her high-level job, care for her child, and began struggling with how to make sense of everything. Her life was fundamentally altered: She has the lasting effects of her medical condition, and she will need to continue to care for her child with special needs on her own. Her emotional pain is ongoing, and she has persistent reminders of her suffering.

Joanna's suffering cuts across multiple themes. First, this unexpected event likely shattered her preconceived plans for her life and thrust her into a sense of groundlessness—she reported significant anxiety and a feeling like life was out of her control. In addition, this was a major disruption in her identity as a career-focused individual, as well as what she had previously thought it meant to be a mother. Her traumatic childbirth was a powerful confrontation with her own death, as well as the potential for her child's death. All these aspects contributed to further pain and suffering.

Heather

At sixteen, Heather was diagnosed with an incurable, chronic, and terminal form of leukemia. The community around her was incredibly supportive; her three closest friends even shaved their heads in solidarity when she lost most of her hair from chemotherapy. Her parents requested an appointment to help her overcome her feelings of depression and loneliness in spite of her supportive community. Given her specific form of cancer and how she was responding to treatments, doctors gave her an expected life span of seven to twelve years, though they warned it could be less. She would commonly say: "People rallied around me when I was diagnosed, but now it's like they don't know what to do with a dying person who is still alive." She reports that she could live for many more years and is not sure what she wants to do with the time she has left. She finds herself not able to talk with her parents because it will often make her mom upset and her dad angry. According to her, they don't like being reminded that she is dying. She feels like she is a burden on the family and that if she would die, life would become easier because the family could just "move on." Heather is unsure if she wants to attend college because she does not want to spend the finite time she has left partying, nor does she want to study for something that she might not be able to do professionally. She reports a few close friendships, but mostly that she does not know how to relate to people her age because they generally like to party and use substances; although she also enjoys these activities, combining them with her chemotherapy treatments can make her incredibly sick. She feels that she "bums" people out when she talks about cancer and doing so causes others to quickly change the subject or end the conversation altogether. Heather finds that she generally makes people uncomfortable with her deep questions, and at the same time thoughts about death and the meaning of life are very present for her. She attended a cancer support group; however, it was largely filled with people who were much older than her. She longs for connection and is unsure how to move forward knowing that she will die. She reported difficulty experiencing and expressing her emotions. Repeatedly, she said she felt "numb."

Heather's medical diagnosis was a direct existential threat. Her two strongest concerns were death and isolation. Death became a reality that she would likely soon face. She felt isolated from her peers and family and was unable to connect meaningfully with others. In addition, she also was wrestling with her new, unwanted identity. All of this manifested in feelings of depression and her secluding herself from her peers.

Matthew

Matthew sought support during college after being released from the hospital following his first Bipolar depressive episode and initial diagnosis of social anxiety. His Bipolar disorder began during his first year in college, and its onset was unexpected and severe. During his first manic episode, he began skipping classes and partying, which led to poor academic performance. Initially, he refused to acknowledge anything was wrong; he didn't want to have the diagnosis of "Bipolar." He avoided the pain of his diagnosis by escaping through drug and alcohol abuse. This was one way he sought to feel "normal." After inpatient hospitalization and a long intensive outpatient program, Matthew was able to acknowledge that he needed ongoing support. He still struggled with the stigma of his diagnosis and felt "weak" that he needed the weekly support of a therapist. He felt out of place when he returned to college a semester behind his peers. His symptoms still recur regularly, and he struggles to come to terms with what his life will look like, often feeling hopeless and even suicidal.

Matthew's suffering was related to his existential questions of groundlessness and identity. The cycles of Bipolar were unpredictable, leading to feelings of loss of control with attempts to gain control through substances, suicidal ideation, or self-harm attempts. He struggled coming to terms with his diagnosis—it was a label, and a life, he did not want.

SHIFTING YOUR PERSPECTIVE

Viewing suffering from an existential perspective can be difficult, and even threatening, because it elicits your own existential fears. Toward that end, we make a few suggestions.

- **Be aware of your own bias.** It is important that you become aware of your own biases or personal leanings that might direct your client's responses to these issues. Your responses are not always the client's responses. So, allow your client the space to feel, think deeply, wrestle, ponder, change their mind, and come to some degree of clarity, or live comfortably without clarity or certainty regarding these issues. No imported or pre-formulated answer will suffice.
- **Explore your own existential questions.** It is helpful to realize that as you work with your clients in their suffering, you may find yourself wrestling with many of these same existential issues. Trafficking in this language and considering these deep questions may lead you to rethink some of your worldview beliefs or may raise your own existential anxiety.
- **Remain patient.** Your work with clients who are suffering may be particularly challenging because we all have a set of defenses that are designed to keep existential anxiety at bay. We encourage you to remain patient, and trust that over time, through building rapport and a strong therapeutic alliance, using the

techniques we describe later in the book, your clients will eventually respond—even though it may take some clients longer than others.

The rest of the book will explore how to apply this framework in each phase of darkness, by focusing on existential concerns and cultivating meaning. We will also show how Joanna, Heather, and Matthew found a flourishing life using our framework. Finally, we discuss ways to help your clients develop sustainable meaning and existential resilience that can withstand the strain of future suffering.

3

Sunset:
The Sting of Suffering

"If your basic outlook is that suffering is negative and
must be avoided at all costs . . . this will add a distinct
psychological component of anxiety and intolerance when
you encounter difficult circumstances. . . . On the other hand,
if your basic outlook accepts that suffering is a natural part
of your existence, this will undoubtedly make you more
tolerant towards the adversities of life."

—DALAI LAMA, *The Art of Happiness*

EACH PERSON EXPERIENCES suffering differently—there is no
one, singular trajectory. However, the experience usually begins with
a sharp sting that sends your client into a phase we call *Sunset*. During
this phase, the core beliefs that have shaped a client's life are tested
against an ill-fitting reality.

Assess/stabilize

In our case, the background from which we viewed and engaged
our suffering was our religious beliefs—beliefs about the fairness and
justice of the world, the nature and character of God, and what is
required to have a good life. When Daryl's brother died, it made us

question a belief that we had assumed was true, namely, that everything happens for a reason. If there was a reason for Tim's death, we realized, it had serious, and potentially devastating, implications about the nature of God. Again, when we were told that we could not have children, it destroyed any remnants of these longstanding beliefs. This made the world seem unfamiliar and scary.

Your clients' beliefs shape their experience of suffering and include the assumptions they bring to therapy and their *cultural worldview*, which is comprised of attitudes, beliefs, expectations, and presuppositions about how the world works. People get stuck in suffering when the erosion of their worldview leaves them prone to the existential anxiety that furthers their distress.

THERAPEUTIC APPROACH

When your clients experience the initial sting of suffering, we suggest two initial parallel clinical goals: *assessment* and *stabilization*. Specifically, (a) engage with your clients in the language of their cultural worldview beliefs, which will help you assess how they find meaning in life, and (b) help your clients stabilize in this period of crisis. Suffering can fragment assumptions embedded in your clients' cultural worldviews, causing them to feel considerable existential angst and despair. Accordingly, it is important to gain an understanding of what clients believe, and how they talk about their beliefs, so you can understand the extent of their shattered beliefs and will know how to frame conversations in terms of existential concerns (when the time is appropriate). In addition, your clients will often be in considerable stress and feel isolated by their suffering. You can help reduce isolation and encourage a safe space to process the suffering by providing a practical presence, validating their enduring pain, and providing coping skills to help them during a crisis. We first discuss research to help you better understand the importance of beliefs, as well as some common beliefs that play a role in suffering. Then, we discuss helpful clinical applications to help you assess and stabilize your clients.

DESCRIPTION AND RESEARCH
Where Most People Start

Shelley Taylor, an expert on how people deal with threatening events, highlights three primary positive illusions that healthy, adjusted individuals hold.[24] First, people have a *desire for meaning*. They like to understand why things happen. In the wake of suffering, people search for meaning as a way to make sense of their pain and loss—however, some suffering eludes easy answers. Clients can get stuck in patterns of thinking that are predominated by forcing their struggles into their prescribed meaning system. This desire can cause unforeseen strain (e.g., trying to make sense of a child's terminal illness while holding the view of a loving and controlling God, or trying to find a "reason" for the suffering, like we tried). Others ruminate on the senselessness of the event, and still others may experience severe anxiety and distress that their beliefs and experiences do not line up. Be attentive to these signs, and realize that, in some cases, it's better for your client to accept not knowing (i.e., uncertainty) than it is to force an answer that is insufficient.

Second, people hold a sense of *mastery* or *control* over their lives, but suffering demonstrates that is largely an illusion. Illness, in particular, makes it clear that people do not even have full control over their own bodies. Your clients may respond to the initial sting of suffering by reporting feelings of a loss of control, or they may react by attempting to re-exert control, even in areas unrelated to their suffering—both of which are tied to an existential fear of groundlessness.

Third, nearly everyone has a strong drive for *self-enhancement*. People like to feel good about themselves and tend to think that they are above average (never mind the fact that not everyone can be above average).[25] Similarly, when things go right, people usually make internal attributions for why this happened and accept the praise (e.g., "I worked hard," "I was an effective therapist"), but when things go wrong, they tend to make external attributions and blame others or the situation (e.g., "My boss is unfair," "My friends are selfish" "My client was resistant to support"). This psychological principle is called self-serving bias.[26]

However, suffering reveals these protective, positive beliefs for what they truly are: *illusions*. No one can explain all of life's events. No one has complete control. And no one is inherently more valuable or better than anyone else. This understanding causes clients to take a sober view of reality, even turning them into *depressive realists*. These individuals see the world as it is and themselves as they are: more objectively and, by default, less positively. In this stage, good work can be done. Your clients can begin to name things honestly. They can talk about their suffering without holding back. Clients might also begin to see the cracks in their long-held beliefs and desire to explore those more fully.

And while this is helpful for gaining a better and more accurate view of the world, such realism comes with a cost. Depressive realists see themselves as average (or worse), they shoulder the blame for their failures, and they estimate that their future, like everyone else's, will be rather ordinary. This can also give way to depression and is one reason why people might get stuck in their suffering.

Taken together, suffering may send many of your clients into an initial state of depressive realism: They feel senseless, out of control, and lack an overly positive self-view. They may feel isolated and may resist wanting to face deeper existential issues for fear of greater depression or mental anguish. Because this depressive realism *can* give way to greater suffering, it is important to prioritize the clients' stabilization, so they can eventually, and courageously, face these deep, pressing existential issues.

The Importance of Worldview Beliefs

Your clients' worldview is a central component of how they deal with existential concerns and is largely what predicts whether people will get mired in suffering or be able to experience flourishing. When provided with relatively objective information, people's beliefs color how they interpret the facts: People are more likely to view ambiguous situations and experiences as supporting their own preexisting beliefs, and they feel more confident that their beliefs are correct, often holding these beliefs more strongly.[27] Your clients' worldview will color how they think and talk about their suffering, will affect the degree to which their suffering is perceived as disruptive, and will play a powerful role in the trajectory of their engagement with it.

Beliefs also direct actions. If your clients believe that they have no control in a situation, they will be unlikely to attempt to change their behavior, viewing such interventions as pointless. If your clients believe God is vindictive and malevolent, they will likely avoid religious practices, religious institutions, or religious people when they are suffering. If your clients believe that everything happens for a reason, they will begin searching ardently for justification in unexplained or unexpected situations, or they may rush to turn a tragedy into a triumph, glossing over the painful truth that should be processed or the injustices that need to be addressed. Understanding your clients' worldviews will help you understand their unique way of interpreting current circumstances.

Shattered Assumptions Reveal Existential Concerns

Going back to the cases we introduced in the last chapter, we can see how the Sunset phase looks for each, and how each client's worldview and positive illusions made the suffering more intense.

- Joanna's career was a central part of her identity; she believed that if people worked hard, they received good and fair outcomes. Moreover, she believed that she could be in control of her future: She had planned everything in her life, and so far, it had worked out "according to plan." However, her traumatic delivery of her child, resulting in her and her child's medical complications, violated these assumptions. It revealed how she was not in control, and it laid bare the myth that the world is fair and just.
- Heather, like most other teenagers, believed that she was invulnerable. She felt entitled to a long life, and she believed that death was an abstract reality to face only many decades in the future. She also believed that God would protect her from harm. Her cancer diagnosis shattered these assumptions and thrust her face-to-face with existential realities of death and isolation.
- Matthew struggled with his Bipolar diagnosis. He assumed that he would have a "normal" life trajectory, and that he would be able to be "in control" of his emotions. His diagnosis, and the reality of the unpredictable and overwhelming nature of Bipolar disorder, pressured these assumptions and left him feeling groundless and anxious.

To best help your clients, you need to better understand their assumptions about themselves, other people, and the world.

Understanding Your Client's Cultural Worldview
Beliefs about Oneself

GROWTH VS. FIXED MIND-SETS. Do your clients believe that they can change, or do they believe that people in general are relatively static? Carol Dweck and colleagues[28] discuss two basic mind-sets: fixed and growth. Those with a fixed mind-set believe that certain traits, abilities, or situations are unchangeable, whereas those with a growth mind-set believe that if they problem-solve or continually work toward developing their skills, they can improve their situation.

Pay attention to the way your clients describe their situations, and the role they play in them. You may probe for your clients' mind-set by asking them how they are coping with their suffering. For example, Matthew explained his choices of isolating himself and alcohol abuse by stating that he is a severe introvert and always has been, and that "that's just how I deal with things," portraying a fixed mind-set. He may not consider seeking social support or widening his relational circle because he says that it "just isn't him" to do so. In the case of Matthew, you might begin by asking, "And how is your 'dealing with those things' going for you?" When your clients approach their suffering from a fixed mind-set, it can be useful to help them identify their own resistance (e.g., "That's just the way I am") before you help them consider another way forward.

Those with a growth mind-set believe that with hard work they can increase their intelligence, abilities, and even their happiness.[29] You can recognize a growth mind-set when your clients believe that their outcomes can change, and they start to take ownership for their progress in therapy. A client with this mind-set may say, "I realize that I've been isolating myself, and that hasn't really been working for me. I think I need to try something new." When your clients have a growth mind-set, you could respond by assigning therapeutic homework to prompt them to enact some change, such as helping them to withstand distress and deal with chronic stressors (explaining that people can grow this aspect of themselves, like a muscle being worked out).

LOCUS OF CONTROL. Locus of control refers to your clients' beliefs about how much agency they have. People with an internal locus of control believe that they are responsible for their outcomes, whereas those with an external locus of control believe that outside forces (whether God, or Fate, or the randomness of nature) determine their outcomes. An internal locus of control can be empowering because people believe that they have the ability to change, whereas an external locus of control may cause people to feel helpless and hopeless.

Discussing control with your clients can be helpful in their initial response to suffering. For example, helping Joanna to acknowledge the things she did not have control over (e.g., her child's traumatic birth and ongoing medical complications) and the things she did have control over (e.g., her response to this suffering moving forward) oriented her toward accepting her situation and starting to engage her suffering in a meaningful way. Because control often cuts across existential themes of suffering, it is important to allow your client to grieve over the loss of control and for you to validate that grief. At times, sessions may end in tears and your client's situation will neither be tidy nor even solvable. In such cases, you could say something like,

> "You have been courageous in naming and feeling your grief around the loss of control you have experienced, and even continue to experience. Although our session time is coming to an end for today, as you leave this space, allow yourself to continue to notice your grief and how this has affected you. We will continue this process together when you come back at the next session. You are not alone in this, and you have shown today that you are able to name your suffering."

When your clients return the following visit, start the session by having them reflect on their experience during the intervening week, what they observed within themselves, and how they experienced the previous session with you. Ask them, in what ways have they become aware of how their grief has affected them and if they noticed anything that surprised them or was a new insight for them in this past week. This new validation in the therapeutic relationship and this emphasis on noticing how their grief has affected them helps provide an initial sense of stabilization and can begin to help them realize where they do have control.

INVULNERABILITY. Most adolescents (and some adults) demonstrate a strong belief in their own invulnerability, that nothing bad will happen to them, and that they are unlikely to suffer personal, lasting consequences for their risky behavior. Heather, for example, knew people who had been diagnosed with cancer, but none of them were young people. If your clients hold the belief of invulnerability, they will be particularly jarred by unexpected adversity or significant trauma—the mere presence of suffering will expose their assumptions about invulnerability.

Because most people buy into this myth of invulnerability, the nature of your clients (e.g., age, developmental stage) and their suffering (e.g., sudden trauma to young person) will affect how your clients view and experience their suffering. You can help normalize the initial shock experienced by your clients when these assumptions are violated. By naming the fears and existential threats that this elicits, it helps your clients to identify the source of their struggle. Again, place your clients' suffering in the context of existential fears—in Heather's case, the fear of death.

Beliefs about Others

To better understand the impact of your client's current distress on their relationships, it is helpful to understand the client's attachment style, which is formed by how their primary caregiver interacted with them during the first few years of life. This serves as a working model for future relationships.[30] Those who received consistent support from a caregiver developed a *secure* attachment style, marked by a trust of others, appropriate boundaries, and the ability to enter healthy relationships. Those raised by a caregiver who was absent or unable to meet their needs developed an *avoidant* attachment style, marked by a distrust of others, rigid boundaries and high defenses, and a pattern of superficial relationships denoted by their lack of intimacy (but often characterized by short-lived casual sexual encounters). Those who received inconsistent messages from their caregivers— sometimes meeting their needs, other times acting with frustration or anger, and still other times being absent—developed an *anxious* attachment style, marked by obsessive jealousy of those they love, inappropriate boundaries (e.g., wanting to merge with close others), and a heightened sense of anxiety and fear of abandonment. You can assess your client's attachment style by asking how they typically relate with other people: Do they consider others trustworthy and safe (secure attachment), clingy and unreliable (avoidant attachment), or distant and unwilling to be as close as they would like (anxious attachment)?

These styles of attachment can be efficiently assessed by asking your client for a brief history of their early life attachment figures (e.g., parents, grandparents, caregivers) and how they perceived these relationships. You can then assess their current relationships as well as their perception of closeness, both before and after the sting of suffering. By paying attention to how they communicate about their relationships, you can gain a greater insight into how they perceive others and how their attachment style might be affecting the relationship. A client who might be anxiously attached may be fearful of rejection from you or might solely rely on your support, forsaking friendships. Heather, for example, typically engaged in an anxious style of attachment and would become highly concerned that the appointments would not be regular if the therapist had a vacation scheduled. She had lost control of her health and was anxious about losing a relationship with the therapist. This was also evident in her perception of how her friends engaged her regarding her illness; she struggled to understand how they could be "so happy" about life (i.e., going to college, dating) when she was dying. A client who might be avoidantly attached may not engage deeply in the therapeutic relationship. For Joanna, it took many sessions before rapport was established and trust was earned by the therapist. She often had engaged in avoidant attachment styles in relationships by solely depending on herself. She had learned to cope this way since she was a young child, and her tragedy challenged her independence. Helping your client to identify how their attachment style might be affecting the way they relate to others, and you, will combat their reaction to isolation and help them gain some autonomy in a world that they are experiencing as chaotic.

Beliefs about the World

The belief in a just world likely provides the overarching structure through which your clients interpret their suffering. If life must be fair, your clients may think that they did something to bring on their suffering. This belief can compound their struggle, as they may feel guilt or shame for something largely outside their control. For example, Joanna wondered whether she could have done something different to change the tragic outcome of her child's health (e.g., genetic testing, different medical care). You will be able to see this in your clients when they get stuck and ask the same questions over and over without a sufficient answer. You can help them by providing a space to address these deep questions that may challenge their underlying beliefs of a just world.

Joanna would often say when she was in session, "I have done everything that was expected of me: I went to school, I got a good job, I worked hard, and I sacrificed. I played by the rules." You could say in response, "Joanna, help me understand what you mean when you say you 'played by the rules.'" Using this approach, you would pay attention to the existential theme of fear of groundlessness. She might be coming to terms with the fact that although she made decisions that she thought would produce an expected and positive outcome, she still experienced pain. In this stage, the therapist is assessing and taking mental notes of when these themes become present, while at the same time validating the pain she is feeling in this initial phase. Joanna is grieving the life she had planned, as well as her realization that she has little control in her life. Her fear of loss of control was becoming apparent in how she was communicating about her health, her child's medical needs, and her career (i.e., "I played by the rules and this happened; I planned everything out and it did not go according to plan."). She is saying she is terrified, and she may be realizing for the first time in her life that she has little control. You might reflect this back to her, and at the same time validate that the loss of perceived control can be terrifying. You are providing a space for her to experience her feelings nonjudgmentally in her current stage of suffering while quietly noting and assessing her existential threats (e.g., groundlessness).

APPLICATION

As in most therapeutic relationships, your clients will look to you to help them when they are struggling. Using the framework that we have outlined—one that is informed by existential and positive psychology—you can *model courage* to ask difficult questions, seek clarification using your *client's language*, and *acknowledge and validate* their pain, while *taking note of their existential concerns*. This requires existential courage on your part. You will not be able to solve the problem of your client's life being cut short from a cancer diagnosis, or fix your client's chronic pain, or alter the reality for your client of having a child born with special needs. As a therapist, your goal is to let go of your own need to control or fix things, and instead bear witness to your client's struggle. The honesty and vulnerability that you show to your clients will directly benefit their ability to be honest and vulnerable with you. Then, they in turn may begin to be honest with themselves. This can be an incredibly transformative process. We provide a few helpful applications of how to engage with your client during this initial phase of suffering.

Start with a Meaning Assessment

To start, work with your clients to assess their meaning, globally and across three dimensions, to get a baseline sense of how meaningful they view their life. Begin with global meaning, asking your client, "On the whole, how meaningful do you feel like your life is right now?" To measure coherence, ask, "What in your life makes sense right now?" For significance, ask, "How much do you feel like you matter right now?" And for purpose, ask, "Do you believe you have a purpose right now?" Doing this models courage to your clients, affirming to them that you hear them and know their suffering has affected them on deep levels. Take note of the language they use, such as references to how they were "before" suffering struck or if the current suffering is exacerbating questions that existed prior to this struggle. Additionally, this interaction can be a helpful bridge to assess for suicidal ideation, intention, or plan. If someone is hopeless, feeling helpless, and expresses that life has limited meaning, you would want to assess for suicidality.

People find meaning across these various aspects, and your client may be experiencing varying degrees of meaning, depending on the domain. Joanna found feelings of significance by becoming a parent. However, the birth of her son resulted in her medical complications and altered her son's life trajectory, which she viewed as senseless and challenged her perception of coherence. Likewise, rather than cultivating a thriving career, her purpose drastically shifted toward caring for her medically fragile son. Overall, Joanna reported that life did not feel very meaningful. Understanding where your clients feel the most and least meaning will help you orient your work with them to cultivate these dimensions where they are low and buttress them where they are high. This can serve as a baseline for your client's meaning, and you can regularly reassess its development throughout your sessions.

Understanding Your Client's Beliefs by Engaging with Cultural Humility

Recall that a central goal is to listen to your clients and use their language when discussing worldview beliefs. One way of facilitating this process is to work to develop cultural humility. Recent research in cultural humility—an awareness of the limitations of one's own way of viewing and understanding the world, coupled with an openness toward and eagerness to learn about the viewpoints of others—reveals that culturally humble therapists have better outcomes with clients.[31] But we have prejudices and stereotypes that shade our thinking, and we are at risk of imposing those prejudices on our clients. You should take care to (a) acknowledge that you are coming from a particular cultural worldview that carries with it a set of implicit assumptions about the world, including some biases; (b) identify your beliefs and biases, and how they might interact with your work with your client (which may require asking trusted colleagues or a supervisor to help you see your own blind spots); (c) generate a desire to know more about your client's cultural beliefs and background; and (d) remain open to feedback about how you may increase your competency in working with clients from various cultural backgrounds and with differing sets of beliefs.

Working to develop cultural humility is important in part because each person's experience of suffering is different, and the aspects of your client's situation that you find troubling may not be what they find troubling. For example, consider a client who is pregnant with a nonviable fetus who elects to carry the fetus to term despite the significant risk it would place on her own health. She holds a strong moral conviction that it is "murder" to terminate the pregnancy, despite the doctor's recommendations to do so. Although this moral judgment may differ significantly from your own, you must be aware of your own personal views and instead engage the client, recognizing and honoring her beliefs.

In this case, the client's primary source of suffering is her feelings of loss surrounding the certain death of her child. Whether she attempts to carry it to term or not, the loss remains. If you focus solely on the intellectual debate around a moral decision, you miss the opportunity to engage your client's beliefs in a way that may foster meaning. This client's commitment to carry her baby to term provides her with the meaning and purpose of allowing her child to die with dignity. For other clients, the decision to terminate the pregnancy could also provide dignity and meaning. So, you must understand the nuances of each client's particular set of beliefs, and why these sets of beliefs are so important to them.

To do this, ask for clarification when necessary and demonstrate to your clients that you want to understand their perspective more clearly. Adopt a posture of openness, curiosity, and learning. You should be receptive to, and seek out, feedback. Ask if you are understanding and reflecting their experiences accurately. Do not perceive their views as a threat to your own beliefs. Your clients may believe in God, when you do not. Be aware of your own defensiveness when discussing existential concerns, knowing that your own assumptions about the world may be (subtly) influencing how you engage your client.

Consider engaging with a client like Heather. During the initial session, she might talk about how she is a part of a strong Christian church community that brings her family meals and checks in with her: Your initial assumption, if left unchallenged, may be that Heather's church community is comprised of like-minded individuals who are a strong sense of support for her. When she expresses feeling isolated, you may instinctively encourage her to become more engaged with people at church. However, in Heather's case this community plays a more complicated role in her suffering—in some cases, increasing her feelings of isolation.

Therapist: Can you share more about your community?

Heather: They've been so supportive and kind to me. I'm grateful to have them, but I don't think they know what to do with me now that I'm still alive.

Therapist: Help me understand: What do you mean by this?

Heather: Well, they're saying that "everything works together for good," but I'm still dying, and it doesn't feel like they understand that.

Therapist: It sounds to me that your faith community is very important to you and yet even when they are trying to support you, you still feel alone.

Heather: Yeah, I feel alone. And I feel guilty because I should feel happy that I have this community and trust that "it will all work out," but I am still going to die.

Therapist: You are faced with the fact of your own death. How do you experience that reality?

These moments, when your clients are engaging existential fears, require you to demonstrate the ability to be open and curious, so that they can begin to voice their authentic feelings.

To help develop cultural humility, it is important to understand that working with clients who are experiencing a life-altering crisis can also be challenging to your own (i.e., the therapist's) expectations of life's unwritten norms. You can ask yourself some of the following questions for a self-assessment: Are you more fatigued, anxious, angry, reactive, or sad after seeing clients with persistent struggles? If so, with which clients? And are there common existential themes that those clients are working through? How have those existential themes interacted with your own life story? Do you find yourself thinking about your clients who are experiencing persistent suffering more than your other clients? This can be explored with intentionality individually, or more formally with supervision or case consultation with other therapists. By becoming comfortable and knowing your own struggles well, you will be able to engage in your clients' struggles with less resistance and defensiveness, modeling courage and resilience.

Helping Your Client Stabilize

PROVIDE A PRACTICAL PRESENCE. The sting of suffering often brings on feelings of isolation. A good start is to offer a practical presence to your client. Your empathic concern may motivate you to quickly alleviate the client's pain (recall some assumptions that you might have about pain and your role as a clinician). Rather than attempt to quickly fix their pain, you could engage your clients in their pain. Remember, this may be the only space in which your clients can be truly honest about what they are experiencing and how they perceive their pain.

First, you should allow your clients to lead the conversation. You should support whatever they wish to talk about and follow where the conversation leads. Second, be sure to offer support to your clients no matter how they present their suffering. Some may come to your office emotionally devastated, whereas others may be covering up their pain and talk about their suffering in a cold, detached manner. Regardless of how they approach, or present, their feelings, meet them where they are. Third, provide your clients with a reliable structure. Much of their life may feel in disarray and could be out of their control. You should allow for therapy to be an area where clients feel like they have control. When possible, offer consistency in scheduling. Communicate clearly if anything changes. Warn the client in advance if you plan to change or cancel any session (e.g., vacation plans, trips). Although these are common therapeutic practices, they are particularly important for a client who is suffering.

Finally, suffering is difficult to talk about. Some people's pain may be so intense that they do not know how to express it. You should allow plenty of space and time for silence, even though you may feel anxious and want to fill the time with reassurances or platitudes. Alternatively, you may want to go deep immediately and find the root of the client's suffering as quickly as possible. Resist both urges. Although clients may appear silent in your office, they may actually be adjusting to the situation. Allow the client to experience pain in a safe and controlled setting, embrace the silence, and offer yourself as a practical presence of support during this isolating season.

It takes bravery to sit with your clients in their suffering and to acknowledge that they walk around with gaping emotional wounds. Doing so may stoke your own fears and challenge your own sense of control; affirming that life is generally out of our control and allowing your clients to experience their pain, rather than alleviate it, may feel excruciating for you.

Going back to the example of Joanna, she sometimes wondered if having a child was a mistake. In response, you could offer, in an affirming tone, "It must be hard to have wanted a child so badly and see the world full of healthy children; to know that life is not what you had hoped for; to know that dreams can go unfulfilled; *to admit that you don't have control.* Being in this space is painful and can feel groundless." However, you must resist the urge to offer your client a false hope or alleviate pain; rather, be quiet and let the client begin to face their own existential fears honestly.

VALIDATE YOUR CLIENT'S EXPERIENCES. Validation is an important part of the early stabilization process. It is critical to listen to how your clients understand their suffering. Even if you have identified certain beliefs that your clients hold, the understanding or expression of those beliefs is most important. In order to avoid making assumptions, ask clarifying questions such as, "Help me understand what you meant by . . ." or "I want to make sure I understand why this is significant to you; can you explain more?" For example, if you know your client is a Christian, that is helpful, but it is not completely informative. To what denomination of Christianity does your client ascribe, or is that not even important to them? Does your client view their religious beliefs positively or negatively? Does your client's view of religion center around shame or freedom? How does your client think God views them? The various beliefs we've discussed are *entry points* to discussions that can help you gain a deeper understanding of how your client experiences suffering.

Validation and alignment with clients will also reduce their defensiveness and help them stabilize after the sting of suffering. You are there, in part, so they do not go through this alone. Suffering can be disorienting and feel foreign. Clients find themselves in unfamiliar situations, having conversations they did not imagine having or planning for futures they never envisioned. Employ active listening to reassure them that they are heard. This can be done by reflecting back their own words to them, carefully homing in on the existential cues in their language. Through your ability to name their deep fears by listening to what they have said, asking for clarification, and summarizing what they have said in existential terms, you are helping reduce isolation by simply being present and saying, "I see your pain too. You are *not alone.* We can go forward and explore this painful place together. You do not have to do it on your own." You are modeling existential resilience and fortitude.

Because of the unfamiliar nature of suffering, many people do not know whether they are reacting in ways that are reasonable or are irrational. Therefore, you should normalize their thoughts and feelings, and be empathetic in all of your interactions. Engage your clients with care and compassion, seeking to understand the weight of their loss from their perspective. But do not pity them, and do not offer unhelpful platitudes or rush to find a silver lining or solution. Many times, your clients will ask questions they think, or hope, require a simple answer. However, the honest response usually deserves an answer that is much more complex. Treat your clients kindly and compassionately, as they are seeking help in one of the most vulnerable times in their life.

In the case of Matthew, his Bipolar diagnosis brought up fears of being seen as weak and damaged. These fears reflected a deeper concern with a loss of (or a drastically altered) identity. Rather than trying to address potentially distorted thinking, which may cause him to feel invalidated, you might say to him:

Therapist: Matthew, it sounds as though you liked who you were before you were diagnosed with Bipolar disorder; you liked that you were strong and independent and could imagine almost doing anything. And since you have been diagnosed with Bipolar, you see yourself as weak and dependent, and you see a limited future. I can only imagine how painful that must feel to you. Have you been able to mourn that you have been diagnosed with Bipolar?

You are affirming to Matthew that he is grieving the life he imagined and the identity that he wanted. You are signaling to him that you recognize his pain. Often, your clients will feel compelled to defend their pain and justify to others that they are hurting; in doing so, they cling to a certain conceptualization of themselves. You are not affirming to Matthew that he is weak; you are, however, affirming that he *sees himself* as weak because of how his changing and unexpected suffering has affected his identity. By affirming the pain your clients feel, even if it is not rational, they will begin to reduce their defensiveness, which will allow them to start laying the groundwork toward accepting the reality of their suffering.

PROVIDE A STRUCTURE. A very practical way to help your clients stabilize is to help them institute a structure into their life. Because the sting of suffering is often disorienting and chaotic, consider providing your clients with concrete steps to organize their lives and help them regain a sense of meaning and purpose. For some clients, this involves simple routines such as meeting with friends two times a week or watching the sunset each evening. More distressed clients may find purpose in the comforting routine of basic self-care, such as having a sleep schedule and taking a regular shower. Once they start finding some structure through building "lower-level" purposes and achieving those goals, they may begin to stabilize.

TEACH DISTRESS TOLERANCE. Many times, your clients may need help increasing distress tolerance in order to help stabilize. It is important that your clients build on their capacity to endure distress and discomfort, especially when such discomfort is outside of their control. The text that follows features several techniques that can be useful to help your clients develop this ability.

Breathing. When your clients are feeling overwhelmed, teaching them breathing exercises can help them in acute phases of distress. In your office, have them practice breathing in deeply for five seconds. Then, have them breathe out slowly for five to seven seconds. They can repeat this exercise three times. This practice can be effective for grounding, reducing panic, and increasing awareness of one's body, especially during active stages of anxiety or panic. The goal is to equip your clients with tools that will allow them to remain engaged when the distress of suffering is particularly high.

Progressive muscle relaxation. During panic or extreme anxiety, your clients can use progressive muscle relaxation. This is another grounding technique that attempts to help them release the energy of anxiety through the tightening and relaxation of muscles. In your office, have your clients engage (tighten) the muscles in their dominant foot. Keeping that muscle tense, have them engage their nondominant foot. Slowly, work up the body, adding both calves, quadriceps, stomach, chest, hand, forearm, biceps, shoulders, neck, and face. Then, have them release the muscles in descending order, starting with the face and ending with the dominant foot with which the process began. Upon completion, they should be a bit tired, but likely more relaxed. (In public settings, an option would be to not include the face in the tightening-release sequence.) This helps your clients release some of the nervous energy elicited by anxiety. They may also want to pair this technique with a word that they find centering such as "peace" or "be" or "openness."

SUMMARY

Each client's suffering looks different. In the wake of the initial shock of suffering, you will need to seek to understand your clients' underlying beliefs about themselves, others, and the world, using their language and approaching them with cultural humility. Learning the nuances of their cultural worldview will help orient you to better see their experience as they see it and understand the sting that is felt at this moment. Establishing a baseline sense of how clients perceive their meaning can be useful to knowing where they feel as though life is meaningful and where they are struggling—which can direct your efforts to help them build meaning across future phases of darkness. Once they are stable from the immediate sting of suffering, they will be ready to further process their suffering and push into the darkness.

4 ⚹

Dusk:
Into the Darkness

"Someone I loved once gave me a box full of darkness.
It took me years to understand that this, too, was a gift."
—MARY OLIVER, *The Uses of Sorrow*

LIKE ALMOST EVERYONE else, we were afraid to push into the darkness. And our processes were very different from each other. Sara almost immediately began to sit with her painful emotions and started to honestly name her suffering within the week of our diagnosis. She spent time alone and in nature, processing what had occurred. Her reactions ranged from tears, feelings of loss and anger, and long nights of sleeplessness, to searching for online support groups and reading books written by authors who were childless but not by choice. She began to use her practice of art to express her sadness and loss. Daryl, meanwhile, buried himself in work and took up long-distance running. And while running helped Daryl take time for himself and process some of his feelings, work was an easy distraction when the feelings became too difficult. Over time, however, Daryl learned that you can't outwait emotions; you have to address them, name them, experience them, and then accept them.

Sunset | Dusk | Midnight | Dawn | Daylight

Acceptance

In the beginning, it can be easier for your clients to try to avoid, numb, or ignore the pain. However, in order for your clients to accept the situation, they must forge into the darkness and experience these uncomfortable feelings. Thus, the primary focus of this phase is to encourage your clients to name their pain, and to give them a space to experience these hurtful emotions without judgment so that they can begin to accept their suffering.

THERAPEUTIC APPROACH

The central goal for your client during this part of the suffering process is to work toward *acceptance*. Your role as therapist is to help your clients by working on two interrelated clinical goals: (a) providing space for them to engage with and experience their emotional anguish, and (b) encouraging them to speak honestly about the true nature of their suffering, including naming their pain. This phase focuses on your clients' emotional experiences. Your clients' first instinct may be to avoid the pain; however, doing so only prolongs their distress and can have other negative consequences. Similarly, if they are not fully honest about the nature of their suffering, it can limit their ability to face their suffering head on. Sadly, people can get lost in isolation when they are unable to name their hurt; shame develops out of this, which amplifies the suffering. Brené Brown's research articulates that "Shame derives its power from being unspeakable" (p. 58, *Daring Greatly*). In this phase, you are helping your clients reduce their shame by being responsive, empathetic, and encouraging them to speak their pain. This silences shame, allowing room for acceptance to take root and begin to grow.[32]

Description and Research

Trying to Cope with Suffering

During suffering, people usually adopt one, or some combination, of three coping approaches. *Problem-focused coping* is when people try to address or fix the source of the stress directly. If they are experiencing stress about a relationship, they will attempt to resolve (or dissolve) the relationship. If they are anxious about an upcoming work assignment, they will productively spend time on the work. This is usually an adaptive response to stress because resolving the stressor should reduce its effects. However, the source of individuals' suffering often cannot be directly addressed or fixed. Joanna, for example, was able to find the best medical doctors for herself and her son, but she was unable to control the outcome of how her body, or her son's, responded to treatment.

When the source of the stress cannot be resolved, people may engage in *emotion-focused coping*. In this option, people attend to their own emotional needs amid stress. The loss of a parent cannot be fixed, but people may seek the social support and care of friends and family in the wake of this loss. When they are sad and grieving, people may write their thoughts in a journal, share their experiences with a friend, or go for a walk to reflect on the ways their lost loved one still lives on in their hearts. Addressing one's emotional needs is healthy and adaptive; however, it is only *one step* in the process of acceptance. When your clients only seek emotional comfort and do not name the depths of their anguish, they may get stuck in a cycle of unproductive emotional comforting or depressive rumination. For example, Heather often skipped school to give herself "spa days" in order to feel better. Although this action provided comfort in a time of discomfort, and may have been needed for a time, she continually relied on this emotional soothing to avoid facing her feelings of isolation from her peers. The balance for your clients lies in being honest about the hurt and the reality of the situation *and* fully experiencing the severity of their suffering.

A third option, one that is decidedly less adaptive, is *avoidant coping*. This is when people simply avoid the stress of their suffering. They disengage, dismiss, or deny the pain. Some sleep too much. Others binge on food, sex, entertainment, or work. Avoidant copers seek to fill every moment with noise that redirects their focus away from their suffering.

Avoiding Pain Makes Suffering Worse

Clients who are already engaged in avoidant coping are also likely to engage in a more general avoidance of unpleasant or unwanted emotions or cognitions, known as *experiential avoidance*.[33] In a study looking at the effects of experiential avoidance in everyday life, researchers surveyed eighty-nine college students daily for two weeks, resulting in more than 1,250 daily diary entries. They found that those who routinely engaged in experiential avoidance of everyday experiences (e.g., avoiding anxiety resulting from commonplace activities) reported less meaning in life and lower well-being each day.[34] This suggests that when people avoid pain, they also miss out on the positive things in life. What's more, a meta-analytic review of studies sampling more than 3,000 participants revealed that experiential avoidance has been linked with depression and anxiety[35] and is associated with psychopathologies such as substance abuse. A qualitative review of twenty-eight empirical studies revealed that individuals who engage in experiential avoidance are more likely to report distress and poorer psychological functioning.[36]

Why do people avoid pain, given the outcomes are so negative? Perhaps the biggest reason is that avoidance, in the short term, feels better than sitting with difficult emotions. It feels good to numb uncomfortable emotions by eating, sleeping, or by losing yourself scrolling through a phone, surfing the Internet, or watching TV. Those small bursts of dopamine are reinforcing, and people chase those small positive responses at the cost of dealing with the deeper issues underlying their misery.

Reviewing the cases of Joanna, Heather, and Matthew, we can see how avoidant coping and experiential avoidance affected them during this stage.

- Joanna struggled to accept her new changes in her body after the medically complicated birth of her son. The stroke had made the left side of her body significantly weaker. Initially, she refused to walk with a cane or attend physical therapy to help her regain and steady her balance. It was not until she fell and injured her knee, requiring additional medical attention, that she began to see that she was denying her body the support that it needed in order to heal. In therapy, this was reflected in the anxiety that she experienced when she tried not to think about her future. She was constantly confronted with it every time she would go to a medical appointment for her or her son. Her relationships with her friends and family began to fracture; she became increasingly angry when her family and friends wanted to offer their time and energy to care for her son. She wanted to care for him on her own, but often was unable to keep up his care due to his specialized medical needs. Soon, agencies such as Child Protective Services (CPS) became involved due to medical doctors' concern that she was unable to care for her son's needs. Joanna was struggling to accept a new reality that she never wanted in the first place.
- Heather had difficulty wrapping her head around dying. She said she often tried to think about it, but she found herself instantly transported to thinking about her anime interest, or the philosophers she liked to read or some new business plan she had developed. Heather said she wanted to feel sad and even to cry, but

she found herself instead feeling "numb" and "empty." Heather could handle managing multiple doctors' appointments and chemotherapy schedules. She was excellent about taking her medication on time. However, when her friends or family would ask how she was doing, she would honestly say, "I don't know." She felt disconnected from herself and from others around her. She found that she was distancing herself from those that she loved, often preferring to focus on her schoolwork or beginning college applications.

- Matthew had endured persistent social anxiety and Bipolar disorder and needed an additional year to finish college. He felt trapped by his persistent anxiety but was resistant to work on the central issues giving rise to his suffering. The only way he felt free from anxiety, and believed that he could connect with others, was when he was drunk or high from chronic marijuana abuse. He withdrew from his friends and started seeking casual sexual encounters, often sleeping with several different women in one week. He struggled to attend classes and maintain his activities of daily living. These avoidant coping techniques not only prevented him from addressing his anxiety and depression, but also led to further suffering: vulnerability to sexual assaults, addiction, a lack of supportive close relationships, and feelings of intense shame.

Not only does avoidance simply not work, it may also create additional distress for your client.

The Importance of Naming the Pain

As we have established, a more direct approach to pain is needed for your clients to flourish. You will need to help your clients fully name their pain, which involves coming to terms with their lack of control.

For Matthew, naming this pain and speaking honestly about suffering involved acknowledging that he had been experiencing anxiety and depression, and did not have the college experience for which he had hoped. Admitting that his life looks drastically different than he had dreamed about is a difficult realization. In the wake of lost control, he tried to assert some level of control over his emotional experience by engaging in substance abuse. Building on the validation of his experiences in the first phase, in this phase, you can help him begin to speak truthfully about his experiences (e.g., realizing his lost dreams) and experience his negative emotions (e.g., persistent anxiety and depression from his unexpectedly different life). Helping Matthew realize the things in life he does not have control over (such as his genetic predisposition to Bipolar disorder and anxiety) and the things he does have control over (such as how he copes with this anxiety and depression) will help him begin the process. Naming, experiencing, and beginning to understand the heartache that life has dealt is a strong first step toward the eventual goal of acceptance.

Overcoming Experiential Avoidance

While naming one's pain is part of the process, there is a need to go beyond that and work to overcome experiential avoidance. Research suggests that through developing *self-regulation*, people can cultivate an ability to engage in difficult but meaningful practices that override their natural instincts for the sake of something bigger or loftier. One way of thinking about self-regulation is like a muscle.[37] In the short term, self-regulation is hard, exhausting, and makes it difficult to practice consistently. But over time, with regular exertion, this muscle builds, and people get better at practicing self-regulation—they can do the hard things that make life meaningful. In fact, some argue that self-regulation helps facilitate meaning in life.[38] This means that one way to help your clients develop and build their self-regulatory "muscle" is through practice. They can start with small decisions to engage in things that make them feel uncomfortable (e.g., exercising a few minutes every day, forgoing dessert once a week), and start building a tolerance for discomfort. In the therapy office, they can work hard to identify, and sit with, difficult emotions as they arise, rather than justify, explain, or rationalize them away. Outside of the office, they can set aside a bit of time each day to check in with their emotions, and then begin to express them either through journaling or sharing (as they feel comfortable) with a trusted friend. Matthew, for example, began to learn how to overcome avoiding pain by weight lifting. He intentionally sought out feeling discomfort by setting a schedule to lift weights every morning. This proved incredibly valuable, as Matthew was able to see how the process of him being uncomfortable as he increased his weights was similar to his process of pushing into his emotional anguish at increasingly deeper levels. It helped him identify a deep determination and a benefit of being uncomfortable—he realized his strength. Over time, both his weight lifting, and his ability to push into the uncomfortable feelings, became more familiar and were not as overwhelming.

APPLICATION

Working with your clients to go into the darkness requires that you actively help develop your clients' motivation and build their capacity to engage with their pain. Acceptance is key. Numerous therapeutic orientations (e.g., Dialectical-Behavioral Therapy [DBT], Acceptance Commitment Therapy [ACT]) have acceptance as a foundational feature of their clinical goals. These various theoretical and clinical approaches suggest that the process of acceptance involves working with your clients to clearly understand the reality of their situation; name their suffering honestly; remain nonjudgmental toward their own emotional experiences; learn to identify, experience, and express their emotions; and allow this emotional information to become part of their story but not solely define it.

Accepting pain is a lengthy process for a client, and it often requires a continued, sustained effort. To help your clients reach acceptance, you will need to resist your urge to fix them; instead, help reduce your clients' defensiveness, and provide them with a space to honestly name, and push into, the pain.

Avoid the Urge to Fix Your Client

When your clients are hurting so deeply from suffering, you may feel a strong urge to fix their suffering, take their pain away, or rush them to a state of relief. For example, with Joanna it might have been easier to focus on her "motivation for treatment" in physical therapy and try to convince her that if she were to go to physical therapy, she would heal more quickly. However, we would be missing the existential significance of her avoiding physical therapy by rationally convincing her that it is what is best for her, and thus denying her the ability to come to that conclusion herself. If we were to rescue her in this way, she might not learn what she needs to help her begin accepting her new reality.

Decrease Defensiveness

No one enjoys suffering, and most of your clients will go to great lengths to avoid it. To help decrease their defensiveness, it is imperative that you develop a strong rapport, adopting a position of nonjudgment. Heather, for example, was isolating herself and did not have a place where, or people with whom, she could talk about dying. Offering genuine interest and pushing into those deeper existential questions shows your clients that you are supportive and on their side. You can use statements that affirm the clients' perspective, such as: "I imagine that if I were in your position, I might feel overwhelmed and fearful. I'm wondering how it feels for you." Your client may mistrust others, God, or the world as a whole, and their doubts may fuel suspicion of therapy and of your abilities and intentions. As they are recalibrating, redouble your efforts to build an empathic setting where they feel safe to fully process the pain and (eventually) engage in existential issues.

When it comes time to discuss existential issues, many clients will find it very difficult to do so. They may be dismissive (*"I don't really see what that has to do with my experiences"*), resistant (*"I don't really want to talk about that"*), deflect and change the conversation (*"Yeah, I guess. Did I tell you about what my boss did last week?"*), or double-down (*"I don't think I'm afraid of being alone at all; I have so many friends."*). However, you can help them by not being afraid to talk about these concerns, but rather engaging them with grace and honesty and treating these issues as unavoidable realities of life. You can even affirm how scary it may be to consider some of these "darker" topics, but also how necessary it is for a complete and whole vision of human flourishing. If you demonstrate an ability to talk frankly and openly about these issues, it will help your client see their importance and that people can discuss them without being defensive or fearful.

It may also be useful to forewarn your clients that defensiveness is a common response. You could start by talking about how *everybody* tends to have certain existential concerns. Then, you could ask them if *they* have ever wrestled with any of those questions. Alternatively, some clients may benefit from more direct attempts to reduce defensiveness. For example, you could say: "I know that this may be difficult, and you may begin to feel a little defensive, but I'm inviting you to consider this question. It may be a tough question, so take a deep breath, and try to remain open." Your clients may alternate between periods of openness and defensiveness; be attentive to ensure you are not pressing too hard, yet continue to challenge them in helpful ways. Ideally, you will keep them engaged in their pain, working to reduce their defensiveness as it arises.

PRACTICE MINDFULNESS. Mindfulness is a receptive, nonjudgmental awareness of experiences, thoughts, and feelings, as they occur, without attaching a label to them.[39] The core tenets are: (a) observing the clients' experience using their emotional and rational processes, (b) describing the situation in an objective manner using their five senses, (c) remaining nonjudgmental, and (d) evaluating what was helpful to the client (or not) without judgment, to apply again in the future. Consider Joanna as she reflects on her many losses. She can observe her inner experiences: anxiety in her stomach, increased heart rate, exhaustion, fear, nervousness, and trouble concentrating. Next, she can describe her emotional and rational responses: Her emotional feeling is anxiety, and her rational explanation is that the reason she is experiencing anxiety is because she is grieving her son's health and her own life. Next, gently remind her not to assign any values or make any judgments on her experience; rather, encourage her to allow herself to feel this way without experiencing shame or guilt for her thoughts and feelings. Doing so will give her permission to not criticize herself for not feeling a certain way (e.g., "I shouldn't be this sad, at least I could have a child") or simply rationalize things away (e.g., "Life is not fair, so I should just get over it"). Rather, she can begin to hold both her emotional experiences (e.g., "I do feel such loss and sadness") and rational thoughts (e.g., "I know nothing in life is guaranteed to be fair") in a way that honors both. Finally, evaluating what in this process worked, and those things that did not work, will help her become more proficient in mindfulness in the future. Remember that this evaluation, too, is completed without judgment.

Encourage Your Client's Process of Pushing into the Pain

As your clients face their pain, they may feel daunted, overwhelmed, and discouraged. Your role is to encourage their process and provide them with objective feedback that will help identify patterns of coping responses that they employ. For example, some clients have predictable cycles of pain-avoidance. Others may start by seeking adaptive responses (e.g., seeking self-care when the discomfort feels too great) that become maladaptive (e.g., using self-indulgence as a way to avoid their pain). Bring these to your client's attention so you can address them in your office. Similarly, affirm their efforts to name their pain and sit with their uncomfortable emotions.

When there is real effort to stop avoiding the pain, have your client reflect on the positive effects of engagement rather than avoidance. For Matthew, drinking reduced his anxiety in the short term, but always led to greater anxiety the next day. One evening, he chose not to drink and instead allowed himself to fully feel his anxiety and used the grounding techniques he learned in the previous phase. As difficult as it was, he felt a bit less anxious the next morning. Taking note of this small change—overcoming avoidance brought on some relief, however minimal—is an important turning point for his process. When your client leans in, provide encouragement. You could say, "Do you see how when you sat with your pain, rather than trying to numb it or avoid it, you survived? You endured. It did not overtake you. Even though it must have been incredibly hard, you were able to bravely face your pain." Be sure to affirm both the client's efforts and achievements in seeking to face this discomfort. Finally, help them find future areas for growth. For example, Matthew can draw from this small victory as he daily has to face a life he did not envision. As deeply ingrained as experiential avoidance is for so many people, the road to fully, honestly, and authentically facing one's pain is equally long and arduous. Let your clients know that it is a process that takes time, and that they can get better at facing the pain.

DIFFERENTIATE BETWEEN UNCOMFORTABLE AND INTOLERABLE. Because of experiential avoidance, many clients may think that any discomfort is intolerable. However, there is a difference between uncomfortable feelings and intolerable feelings. When your clients are feeling distress, ask them to rate the discomfort on a scale from one to ten, where one is mild distress or discomfort, and ten is the most distress or discomfort the client has ever experienced.[40] The majority of the time, the majority of clients will respond with a number that is seven or below, which is uncomfortable. Uncomfortable experiences need to be engaged. To do this, ask your client to sit quietly in your office and take stock of what they feel in their body, and where they are experiencing these feelings. Allow them a few minutes to simply experience these bodily sensations. Then, ask them to describe what they felt, and where they felt it. Then, you can ask them to identify what emotion they think it is related to, and how this emotional experience may be related to their suffering. This process can be repeated many times.

There are individual differences in how clients perceive their distress or discomfort; for example, some will consistently rate any discomfort as a nine or ten. Ratings higher than seven require distress tolerance, with temporary breaks—perhaps redirecting the therapy session for a few minutes (or teaching them how to distract themselves for a short time when trying this practice at home). However, it is important for your clients to return to their negative feelings. Over time, their capacity to endure will grow, and they will be able to withstand greater discomfort. Some clients will learn these skills in a session or two; for others, you may need to spend more time here. This is an essential skill for wading into the darkness of suffering.

Another assignment that can help your clients engage with the uncomfortable is to have them perform some mild physical exertion that increases their heart rate and breathing. Assess your client's physical condition and ability; if your client is able, assign homework for physical exercise. A brisk walk could be enough to increase their discomfort. For others, taking a more challenging exercise class or increasing the speed, length, or duration of their running, biking, or exercise regimen may be sufficient. The goal is to create a situation in which clients persist, even when it feels uncomfortable, and to develop a greater awareness of their body's responses. This will help them discover that they can persist and remain resilient in the face of uncomfortable, and perhaps unsettling, experiences.

COMPLETE A COST-BENEFIT ANALYSIS OF PUSHING INTO THE PAIN.

Clients who are consistently at an eight, nine, or ten in distress may need to take a session or two to consider the benefit and the cost of pushing into their pain.[41] Your role is to help your client make the costs tolerable or give them skills to turn those costs into benefits. For example, a cost of experiencing high levels of discomfort may be an increased frequency of panic attacks in the short term—this was the case for Heather. You can first help clients make this cost tolerable by teaching them coping skills to endure the panic attacks, making them slightly less costly. Crucially, you can help your clients see that while experiencing discomfort may lead to panic attacks in the short term, directly addressing the core issues of their suffering may likely decrease the frequency of their panic attacks altogether in the long term.

When Heather did a cost-benefit analysis, she mentioned that some of the costs included "panic attacks, anxious feelings in her stomach, sadness, feeling overwhelmed, and that facing the pain is exhausting." When asked about some potential benefits of facing her pain rather than avoiding it, she mentioned: "not being controlled by fear, actually starting to feel things again besides anxiety, and being able to be around friends and family who are having fun." With Heather, mitigating costs involved identifying grounding techniques for her anxiety that would help her cope with the panic attacks and negative emotions. Also, in doing this, Heather saw that the freedom of not being controlled by fear and the connection with friends and family outweighed the anxiety and panic she felt. This helped motivate her to address her suffering rather than avoid it.

RADICAL ACCEPTANCE. Radical acceptance is indeed *radical*—it's a seismic shift in the way your clients think about their suffering. Radical acceptance is a therapeutic technique, borrowed from the DBT tradition, in which clients who are faced with a reality that cannot be changed must endure the hard work of altering the way they think about their suffering to plainly accept their current reality.[42] It bypasses denial, minimization, and rationalization to get your clients to live in the reality of the true nature of their suffering. Thus far, we've explained acceptance from an emotional perspective (i.e., experiencing the depths of one's hurt, loss, and grief). Radical acceptance is a cognitive choice. This change in cognition gives way to the cognitive work that begins in the next phase.

In the therapy session, you can provide your clients with psychoeducation on radical acceptance: the opportunity to speak honestly about the true nature of their suffering and live in the reality not of what they want or desire, but what *is*. For Joanna, after grieving her child's medical condition and the lost dreams of what she had hoped parenthood might look like, she was left with the choice to accept her reality: She and her son had severe medical needs that required attention. Through intentional cognitive work, she stopped minimizing their effects or believing she could handle it all on her own, and she saw clearly the significance of her suffering. This led her to reach out for assistance for herself and her son, communicate more clearly with doctors, and make a reasonable and realistic plan for her future. She was done denying and rationalizing it away—now she was living firmly in the reality of her suffering. And by doing so, CPS reduced their involvement. Only after she was able to radically accept the reality of "what is" was she able to cope with it. This capstone feature of acceptance helps ensure future work will lead to flourishing in suffering.

SUMMARY

Many of your clients will want to avoid their pain. This experiential avoidance will keep them from engaging in the hard work of addressing the root causes of their suffering. Your focus, after having helped them stabilize during the last phase, should be to help them work toward acceptance. You are inviting your client to name their pain and begin to experience some of those difficult and uncomfortable emotions. To do this, you can help them decrease their defensiveness and begin to lean into the hurt and grief. You will help them build a tolerance for engaging directly with some of their existential questions and fears. As they increase their ability to experience discomfort, you will encourage their progress and equip them for the steps ahead. Through this, you are beginning to model the courage to suffer.

5

Midnight:
The Deconstruction Process

"There is no birth of consciousness without pain."
—CARL JUNG, *The Development of Personality*

IS GOD GOOD? Does God even care about us? Or are we just a part of some plan concocted by a selfish God who is indifferent about our well-being? In fact, does God even exist at all?

We asked these questions after squarely facing, naming, and accepting the pain of our situation. And the questions scared us. Going forward, we had a choice: We could simply give these questions a cursory treatment and move back into our original, predominant beliefs, or we could start questioning *all* of our beliefs to see which held up to our new reality and which did not. We forged ahead with questioning and started to deconstruct our beliefs.

Active questioning

If your clients face and accept their pain, this encounter usually allows them to deconstruct their beliefs. For some of your clients, this stage is as far as they are willing, or ready, to go in the process. Thus, they may terminate your services and leave therapy, thinking that they have worked through these issues enough.

However, for those who allow deconstruction, this fork in the road will lead them toward an unknown path marked with resilience, potential growth, and adapted beliefs. They will begin to reshape their beliefs in ways that honor the reality of their suffering. Richard Rohr, a Franciscan priest and spiritual teacher, suggests that the "falling" that occurs through suffering (which may feel like experiencing spiritual lows or despair) is actually a necessary part of reaching new spiritual heights.[43] This deconstruction phase may be the hardest part of the suffering process, both for the client and for you—largely, because it requires directly confronting existential concerns.

THERAPEUTIC APPROACH

Some clients will end therapy at this stage partly because they have reached a brief sense of resolution with their pain, and partly because they are so worn down by the process of suffering. Inviting more doubt, uncertainty, and existential angst into their lives can feel overwhelming. Accordingly, most therapeutic approaches only bring clients through the first two phases of darkness and no further. For example, CBT may address some of your clients' distorted thoughts, but does not require a full-scale examination of their implicit assumptions about the world, let alone the existential ramifications of challenging such beliefs. In our view, such approaches are incomplete. Future suffering will occur, and your clients have the opportunity now to build resilience by questioning—and deconstructing—beliefs that have not held up to the reality of their suffering. The central goal of this phase is *active questioning*. You can help your clients question some of their central beliefs (which you identified in the first phase) considering their pain and suffering (which they accepted in the second phase). Often, this results in a dismantling of, at least some of, their beliefs.

DESCRIPTION AND RESEARCH

When your clients deconstruct their beliefs, they are left to face the full anxiety elicited from confronting existential concerns of death, groundlessness, isolation, identity, and, ultimately, meaninglessness. This may lead them to feel as though they are getting worse or regressing in therapy, at which point they may become suicidal or report feelings of hopelessness. Be very aware of these possibilities.

In addition, this process will likely also be hard for you. Your client's deconstruction of beliefs may raise a new iteration of your own questioning. This is why we strongly encourage you to examine your own beliefs and seek supervision or support along the way. This is where courage is necessary: both regarding your drive to stay in the hard and painful places with your clients (rather than react defensively) and your clients' courage to question their central beliefs.

- Joanna, as you might recall from Chapter 3, believed in a just world: a world in which those who worked hard and did the "right" things received good and fair outcomes. She believed that by planning for everything and making the right decisions she could avoid unnecessary hardships. When her son was born with special medical needs and she had a traumatic birthing experience, this belief was challenged. She initially resisted this reality (Chapter 4) and CPS became involved. Through the process of naming her pain, decreasing her defensiveness, and engaging in acceptance, she was able to accept her current reality. And by doing so, her original belief in a just world was challenged. After acceptance, Joanna was again faced with her existential fears of groundlessness (lack of control), identity (career), and ultimate fear of death (for both herself and her child). During the initial stages of deconstruction, Joanna felt hopeless and helpless. Often, she would say, "What is the point, anyway? I can work hard and have a plan, but now it can all be taken away." She was in the depths of deconstruction, and she was trying to make sense of her struggles.

- Heather's predominant worldview centered around her invulnerability, which stemmed in part from her religious beliefs that God would protect her. She expected, as most adolescents do, that death was not a worry for many decades to come. Her diagnosis of leukemia challenged this assumption. It exposed her fears of death, challenged her identity, and plunged her into isolation. As a result, she feared her future death, had to renegotiate her identity of what it meant to be a young person with a terminal diagnosis, and felt disconnected from those she loved. After she realized that she was using her schoolwork to avoid these fears, she was able to accept her diagnosis, which left her facing the existential threat of death. She felt overwhelmed by the idea of dying and was not sure how to go forward.

- Matthew's diagnosis of Bipolar disorder and his lived experience of mood shifts were shattering to his identity. His belief that he should have a "normal" life and mastery over his emotions resulted in increased substance use to better exercise control over his emotions. Once he reached acceptance, he began to grapple with the reality of his Bipolar disorder and substance use. He was often suicidal because he could not see how he could continue to live with the roller coaster of emotions and unpredictability of his mood, while trying to navigate school, relationships, and eventually a career. His acceptance of his diagnosis exposed the existential threats of identity and fears of groundlessness.

For us, the deconstruction process may have been the hardest part of our suffering, and we still feel the effects today. After our deconstruction process, we lived with more uncertainty and less clarity about how life "should" look. Our identities not only as parents, but also Christians, were now unclear. Our friends settled into parenthood, yet we felt aimless and isolated. In a society that provides a map for cultural expectations of meaning—college, graduate school, launch a career, get married, have children, raise your kids, and then help raise grandchildren—we suddenly had no compass. Our views of God were also eroding. Whereas Christians typically draw comfort from some spiritual assumptions—certainty of beliefs, faithfulness of God, the goodness of God, the existence of God, and prosperity in belief—we felt devoid of a larger meaning and were forced to make changes to what we believed, simply because our reality no longer matched what we believed. It felt like the darkest period of suffering.

The Discrepancy-Distress Dilemma

Crystal Park has developed a "meaning-making model" for understanding how people make meaning in the wake of adversity or trauma.[44] People tend to evaluate reality against their expectations. When there is a discrepancy between the two, they often feel distress. For example, some see the loss of a loved one as a failure of the Divine: How could God let this happen? How they come to make sense of their suffering is juxtaposed against their global beliefs or meaning system. Most people believe that God is loving and protective. However, suffering can cast doubt on this belief. Thus, the discrepancy between the perceived reality that God allowed, or perhaps caused, their loved one to die and their expectation that God should be loving and protective creates distress. The distress your client feels is usually proportional to the degree of the discrepancy; bigger discrepancies elicit more distress. For Heather, once she accepted the reality of her terminal diagnosis, she experienced a considerable discrepancy between this truth and her beliefs regarding her invulnerability and a protective God.

Meaning Erodes in Deconstruction

Recall that meaning is comprised of coherence (i.e., making sense of the world), significance (i.e., the feeling that you matter), and purpose (i.e., having a direction in life). The deconstruction process makes it difficult to find meaning across these dimensions. The ability to make sense of the world is a key feature of a flourishing life, and the process of deconstruction can take that ability away, leaving your client vulnerable, afraid, and angry. Moreover, your clients may isolate themselves or may be isolated by others who are suspicious of their doubt and changing beliefs. For example, Heather did not feel as though she belonged in her faith community as she doubted her spiritual beliefs, and she experienced ostracism from those who once offered support. This caused her sense of significance to crumble. Others suddenly feel aimless and without a purpose. When you notice your clients' meaning erode, it does not mean anything is wrong—rather, they are engaging in the hard, necessary work of this phase.

Beliefs Are Notoriously Difficult to Change

Engaging your client in active questioning is important, but, at times, it can be challenging and frustrating. Beliefs are very resistant to change. Even when evidence suggests that they should change, people do not like to do so. A common term for this phenomenon is belief perseverance.[45] When the objective world clashes with one's subjective beliefs, people usually *assimilate* their experiences: They interpret their experiences in a way that fits with and preserves their preexisting beliefs. So, when you are inviting your clients to engage in active questioning of their beliefs—by comparing their worldview and beliefs with the reality revealed by their suffering—they may defer to interpret such experiences in ways that are consistent with their long-held beliefs. This does not lead to deconstruction, but rather will leave your client in a similar situation to when the suffering initially stung.

However, because your clients' experiences most likely cannot be assimilated into their belief structures, your goal is to help your clients *accommodate* their beliefs: this requires altering their beliefs to fit reality. This accommodation involves belief deconstruction, which is precisely where so much powerful work occurs. The hope is that through active questioning, you can guide your clients toward deconstruction.

Deconstruction as a Search for New Meaning

The *search for meaning* is when people attempt to recover lost meaning or find meaning in different areas in life. As it relates to suffering, we contend that, for many, this process involves the deconstruction (and eventual reconstruction) of their beliefs. Research on both personal and collective trauma related to finding meaning reveals three important truths.[46] First, most people search for meaning. Second, *finding* meaning is key. Those who search for meaning but cannot find it fare worse than those who search for and find meaning. In fact, those who do not search for meaning tend to have better outcomes than those whose search is unsuccessful. This means that embarking on the process of deconstruction, which is part of the search process, will lead to better outcomes, but only if they are able to find meaning by reconstructing their beliefs. A perpetual state of deconstruction can adversely affect well-being and functioning. Third, finding meaning early in the process predicts positive trajectories. Those who languish and do not address how their adversity has affected their sense of meaning have poorer outcomes than those who cultivate meaning early on. The longer people wait to search for and reestablish meaning, the harder it will be for them in the long term. Similarly, staying in a state of meaninglessness can have deleterious effects.

Balancing the Burden

For these reasons, it is vital to help your clients balance the burden between languishing in and rushing through the deconstruction of their beliefs. If your clients remain too long in deconstruction, their meaning will continue to erode, and their mental health may deteriorate. However, deconstruction takes time. To rush the process could result in (a) an incomplete examination of their beliefs, (b) the replacement of their beliefs with inadequate or unexamined new beliefs, or (c) the adoption of beliefs that are not authentic or do not genuinely align with their values or honestly reflect their experience of suffering, all of which will only prolong your clients' suffering. Thus, you must help your clients remain engaged, yet not stagnant, in deconstructing their beliefs.

Mindfulness and grounding techniques should continue throughout all phases of suffering when any part of the process becomes too distressing. Similarly, your clients can remain steadied in the deconstruction process by identifying and building other sources of meaning in life. Encourage your clients to find social support and remain engaged in close relationships, and to connect with something larger than themselves. For many clients, this can involve nature, or meditative practices such as yoga, or artistic expressions through music or creating. Matthew started taking a pottery class, which provided him with a sense of structure, allowed him to make new connections, and gave him an opportunity to create when he was in the process of actively deconstructing so many of his beliefs. This provided balance and allowed him to experience flourishing, even while he was still suffering.

APPLICATION

Recall that the goal of this phase is to help your clients engage in active questioning. If your clients can genuinely engage in thorough questioning of their beliefs, they will begin to rid themselves of whatever does not feel authentic and revise their beliefs (which we discuss in the next chapter). This is why making sure they have honestly named and experienced their pain in the previous phase is so important—without doing so, they cannot accurately assess which beliefs are misaligned with the reality of their suffering.

This phase can feel like the "in-between," which is a helpful phrase to describe when your clients struggle with old ways of viewing the world but have not yet settled on new sets of beliefs or identities. When Heather asks the question "What's the point?" and does not have an answer yet, she feels groundless and uncertain. However, in this space, she can explore a genuine and authentic response that honors her suffering. This concept of "in-between" can be a useful distinction from other approaches, such as CBT, where the goal is to find concrete answers to questions in order to correct one's thinking.

Going Beyond the Symptoms

Your clients typically come to therapy wanting to learn coping skills or reduce their overall anxiety, depression, or strained relationships. Your goal in this phase is to help them shift from thinking solely about *symptoms* to also considering the *deep roots* that give rise to these feelings, and how their beliefs are contributing to these. This is not to say that you should ignore your clients' symptoms. Rather, you can help them identify these deeper causes of their suffering by pointing toward the existential threats that underlie their symptoms. For example, a chronically ill client may be experiencing anxiety and sadness about her impending death. She fears that her husband and small children will not be well cared for. She is angry at the fact that her children will have few memories of her. All of these feelings are justifiable and reasonable. But what might be the root cause of these distressing feelings? You can ask her if her struggle with existential themes of isolation, lack of control, and, most notably, death may be causing distress and manifesting in feelings of anxiety, sadness, and anger. You might help her identify that her belief that the world is fair may be causing her even more distress. You can help her engage with the existential realities of death and isolation by acknowledging their unavoidable reality and encouraging her to think about which of her beliefs are worth keeping. Would she feel more authentic and genuine to her experiences of suffering if she discarded or revised some of her beliefs?

ENGAGE IN EXISTENTIAL QUESTIONING. One of the ways to go beyond merely treating the symptoms is to use existential questioning. You may begin by making gentle connections between your clients' experiences and deeper existential questions or fears they may have. You may need to provide some education about the core concerns of groundlessness, isolation, identity, and death (and how they all can erode meaning in life). As you make connections, invite your client to *go deeper* in their explanation. *Why* does the loss of a loved one hurt so badly? Does the unpredictably of life feel terrifying? Are they fearful of being alone? Do they fear their own death? Most clients will provide responses that on the surface are justifiable and reasonable. However, many of their reasons for fear, anxiety, or depression may stem from deeper, unresolved existential concerns that are now in their mind. Begin to make these connections as you lay the groundwork for future sessions.

Heather: I've been feeling really frustrated at my friends. They're all applying for college. Specifically, my best friend. She's gotten into a college that has a great pre-med program, and that's all she's talking about. I know I should be happy for her, but it's pissing me off.

Therapist: Tell me about your frustration.

Heather: I don't know. I guess she just keeps going on and on about college and medical school and about being a doctor someday. It's just getting under my skin.

Therapist: Tell me about how it is getting under your skin.

Heather: So here we are, we have been best friends our whole lives and take almost all the same classes. She gets to dream about going to medical school and will be a doctor around the time that I am planning my own funeral.

Therapist: It sounds to me that you are struggling to make sense of how your life has taken a different turn from your friend's. That this might be bringing up not only your own fears about dying, but also trying to navigate what your identity might look like as most of the people your age are going off to college. I can only imagine how isolating it must feel as your friends are moving forward without you.

Heather: Yeah, I always saw myself going to college, and definitely not dying young. In fact, I thought I would grow old. You know, God looking after his children and all. I don't know what I am supposed to do with my "seven to twelve years" I have left.

Therapist: Heather, are you angry with God—that you weren't protected?

Heather: Well . . . I guess, kind of. I mean, what's God doing letting a teenager get cancer anyway? Doesn't the Bible say that God protects his people? I mean, that is what I was taught anyway.

Therapist: Well, in light of everything that has happened what do you think about that?

Heather: As much as I want to believe it, it sure doesn't feel that way right now. So, yeah, I'm kind of mad at God, honestly.

Taking the opportunity to direct your clients back to these core existential issues will help them grapple with how those beliefs are serving these deeper purposes, and identify which beliefs may need to be evaluated.

CHALLENGE THE LOGIC OF SOME BELIEFS. Another helpful technique to facilitate deconstruction is to challenge the logic of your clients' beliefs. This begins by asking your client to think about how they developed the beliefs in the first place. Some beliefs were passed on from parents. Others were learned from religious upbringing. Some simply were observations of how others interacted with the world and assumed this way was naturally correct. You should gently, but directly, question the logic of such beliefs. Point out their inconsistencies. Highlight their unintended distressing consequences. Ask your clients to provide evidence for their beliefs. After careful examination, some beliefs will hold up to scrutiny and others will not, requiring that they be revised or discarded. This can be a "start-stop" process that unfolds over time. Moreover, you will be modeling the process of existential courage and curiosity that you hope your clients will employ on their own, outside of your office.

Therapist: Can you tell me, Joanna, about where you might have first learned the belief that you have told yourself for so long, "If you work hard, you can control your outcome in life"?

Joanna: I don't know, I guess this was just always a part of my family's values growing up. They really pushed us to work hard.

Therapist: So, this has always been a part of how you see the world?

Joanna: Yes, I think I've believed this since I was young.

Therapist: And it sounds to me like it has worked for you: You have been successful in your career, have become very independent, and have worked toward a goal. I could imagine that this was adaptive for you growing up and may even be a reason why you worked so hard growing up.

Joanna: Absolutely. This belief has worked well. And I still value hard work.

Therapist: Sometimes things that were adaptive for us when we were younger stop being helpful or even become maladaptive. What do you think about that belief in light of the traumatic birth of your son?

Joanna: Hmmm. I'll need to think about that. I suppose that believing that if I just worked hard enough that things would turn out my way did not really pan out. I mean, I did everything right, and all of this still happened.

This can provide a launching point for your clients' own active questioning of this belief.

Encourage Your Client's Intellectual Exploration

Challenging and deconstructing beliefs can be frightening for people, and a significant amount of inertia may be working against them. For instance, friends and family may tell your clients that they should not question certain core beliefs, making them feel guilty or hesitant. Often, the beliefs themselves are so ingrained that they are very hard to change, even when your clients are motivated to do so.

Ultimately your clients must give themselves permission to engage in honest intellectual exploration of their beliefs, but sometimes you have to give it to them first and encourage them (in a way that feels authentic and in a manner that fits their style) to seek new perspectives that challenge their longstanding views. A number of cognitive therapies ask the client to "reason against themselves." By doing this, your clients are encouraged to think of alternatives or different outcomes beyond the assumptions or beliefs to which they are committed. This type of "detective thinking" opens up new, more accurate, and more honest ways of approaching their suffering.

You can also serve as the outside voice of alternative perspectives. However, this requires that you continue to engage in your own intellectual exploration. You may find your clients' journey into deconstruction unsettling if they question, doubt, or discard beliefs that are central to you—ones that organize your life and provide you with meaning and purpose. In such cases, you might feel motivated to defend those beliefs out of your own need for self-protection. Remember, however, that your beliefs may accurately represent your experiences and are likely operating well for you. Therefore, remain culturally humble and tailor your engagement specifically for each client.

Keep Your Client Grounded

As your clients explore their own beliefs and seek out new ones, they may experience a high degree of existential anxiety. You can help them remain grounded in simple and practical ways. Building on what you and your client have practiced during the Sunset phase, remind them to build their distress tolerance and to practice being uncomfortable (and the benefits that arise from this discomfort). Remember, your clients can establish a sense of control in their lives by devising a routine and sticking with a schedule. Even smaller instances of structure, such as waking up at the same time or working out before dinner, may provide comfort as their existential anxiety reaches its peak.

PROMOTE SELF-CARE. One sure way to keep your clients grounded is to help promote their self-care. Deconstruction is taxing, exhausting, and anxiety-provoking. Continue to encourage them to seek out ways to nurture their self-care, such as through exercise, immersing in nature, or enjoying meditation or yoga. In addition, your clients' old ways of caring for themselves may not be as helpful as they once were. For example, a client who is struggling with her views of God may no longer find church to be supportive or encouraging. Those who have lost a child may not find comfort in spending time with friends who have children. It will be helpful to aid your clients in identifying new ways for self-care amid their deconstruction. Whereas in the early phases of suffering, self-care is designed to help people cope with the immediacy and severity of their pain, in this phase, self-care is designed to keep them grounded and connected to the broader world around them. For example, Matthew used to lift weights to help reduce his early distress; in this phase, his pottery class helps him create and ground himself in his body. This self-care might look very different than how they cared for themselves during the initial sting of suffering.

SUMMARY

The discrepancy between people's beliefs and their experiences generates much of the distress of suffering. As your clients deconstruct their beliefs to more closely align with their new understanding of the world, they may be consumed with feelings of loss and meaninglessness. Your role during this process is to help guide their active questioning, while affirming and grounding them, even with the reassurance that this groundless feeling is signaling that they are exactly where they need to be. This will help them refine which beliefs are helpful and worth keeping, and which beliefs need to be revised or discarded. Finally, you can continue to direct your client to the existential concerns and questions that underlie much of their suffering. This deconstruction is terrifying, but you can help model the courage necessary to flourish in the midst of this phase of suffering.

6 ⚹

Dawn:
The Reconstruction Process

"Psychological wholeness and spiritual holiness never
exclude the problem from the solution. If it is wholeness,
then it is always paradoxical, and holds both the dark and
light side of things."
— RICHARD ROHR, *Falling Upward*

AS TERRIFYING as the deconstruction process may be, reconstruction can be empowering. We rebuild after storms wreak havoc on our homes; we search for life after the earthquake hits; we scour the ashes after fire scorches the earth. Humans rebuild. It's our human nature to adapt, and our survival depends on it.

Reconstruction takes time to unfold. You cannot, and should not, rush this process. It also depends, largely, on how much your clients have been able to push into the pain and honestly name their suffering. In our story, we had different trajectories. Sara was able to move into and through deconstruction and reconstruction because she was able to accept the pain more fully and honestly. In addition, her work with clients often required her to push into own discomfort and face her own fears. Because Daryl didn't fully embrace the pain but rather engaged in avoidance, his deconstruction process was harder and less sustainable. Only slowly, and more recently, did Daryl push more into the process of questioning, deconstructing, and reassembling beliefs. Thus, even though we went through the same crisis, we reacted and engaged very differently. It is important to keep this in mind as you work with your clients. Individuals vary in how they react and engage suffering. Your role is to help them rebuild when they are ready.

Autonomy

THERAPEUTIC APPROACH

The central focus of this phase is to encourage your clients to develop *autonomy*. This is accomplished by (a) facilitating a spirit of openness and curiosity; (b) encouraging your clients to begin to rebuild a set of beliefs, however tentative, that address existential concerns; and (c) helping your clients adopt a narrative that is consistent with their story of suffering. By allowing clients to actively author their own story, rather than react against it, they are able to demonstrate autonomy and reframe their experience so that their suffering is incorporated, but not the defining element. This can be incredibly empowering.

It is important to note that reconstruction can reengage the fear of groundlessness in a new way. As your clients are reframing their worldview, they lack the certainty that these beliefs are "correct." Many may feel guilt for walking away from beliefs that they may have held since childhood. This can cause feelings of anxiety and uncertainty, because your clients don't know what the "right" choice is, and they must choose out of countless options. This, too, is a direct confrontation with their existential fears.

Reconstruction does not mean that your client now has all of the answers. For most people, it involves living in the tension that they do not have the answers, and such a posture can still be settling and comforting for them. They can grow to learn to live with uncertainty and the potential anxiety that this brings. This requires a shift not only in beliefs but also in their narrative. Moreover, it requires a change in their posture toward existential concerns of being more open and less defensive.

Reconstruction is a process. It may continue as people move into the next phase—dawn bleeds into daylight. Your clients do not have to complete this process fully for it to be authentic. Although some people will want to rush through this revision process, it is important for your clients' existential resilience that they do not move too quickly. They must take the time necessary to build a set of beliefs and tell their story in a way that is true to their suffering. The revision process can be a lifelong practice.

DESCRIPTION AND RESEARCH

Deconstruction leaves people fully prone to existential anxiety. If people remain at that stage, they languish. However, you can guide your clients through the work of revising their beliefs. Although this process is challenging, it is also empowering and freeing, and revision can begin to provide real, lasting, and sustainable relief from suffering as your clients shape beliefs in ways that more genuinely reflect the reality of their suffering.

- Joanna worked hard to abandon her longstanding belief in a just and fair world and was mired in a sense of meaninglessness, questioning what the point of life is, given her lack of control (during deconstruction). Left with this void of how to make sense of the world, in therapy, she began to explore why she was motivated to have a child. Rather than presume it was because it felt like the "right thing to do," or because she could control her life, she realized that this desire to have a child was motivated by love. And even though she did not have the child she dreamed of or in the way she had hoped, her love for her child was stronger than ever. She began to replace her belief in a fair and just world that offered her a sense of control with a view of herself and a narrative of her own life story, shaped by love. By reorienting her story from control to love, she anchored her fear of groundlessness and provided herself with a new identity that is authentic to her suffering. Doing so helped her quell her existential concerns and regain a sense of meaning and purpose (e.g., taking care of and loving her son).

- After having turned inward for so long and being unable to make sense of her faith in light of her suffering, Heather began to explore new ways of relating to God, and others. She started to think differently about her death—not as a ticking clock counting down her days, but rather as a reminder that life is precious and short and beautiful. She replaced her assumption of invulnerability and protection with an understanding that life is finite and something to be cherished. She may not be able to control how her life ends, but she started learning to think differently about the time she has left. This changed her identity from being a "cancer patient" to being "intentional and fully human." She became more comfortable with the existential reality of death (and the residual anxiety that accompanies it) as she addressed her shifting identity. And viewing her diagnosis as part of her larger story motivated her to think differently about how to engage and include her friends, which reduced her feelings of isolation.

- Matthew's shift from deconstruction to reconstruction was subtle. Recall, his pain originated from the mismatch of his beliefs about what it meant to be "normal," and his lack of control over his emotions. He assumed that a Bipolar diagnosis was akin to a "death sentence," effectively ruining his life. Once he relinquished his beliefs about what it meant to be normal, and admitted that life could not be controlled, he replaced those beliefs with slightly different ones that helped set him free. He realized that his diagnosis was not damning, and he could, in fact, have a full life after he better understood himself and his Bipolar experiences. Also, he came to understand the things he could have control over and started to invest in those, reducing his fears of groundlessness. This helped him rewrite his narrative in a way that brought his suffering in line with his strength and resolve, helping address his fears of an uncertain identity. His new view of what it meant to be normal, and his revised view of his life's trajectory, gave him the autonomy and freedom to create a future in which he was flourishing.

Understanding how to shift people from a state of deconstruction to reconstruction is a key transition to helping your clients flourish, especially when their suffering cannot be resolved.

Revising Beliefs

Deconstruction highlighted the discrepancy between one's beliefs and experiences, which is why that phase is so distressing. To reduce that distress, the client must adopt new beliefs that align with reality.

Belief revision is a broad term, but two primary changes occur in the season of reconstruction: a change in the *content* of their beliefs, and a change in the *style* of their beliefs.

Most basically, your clients may change what they believe—the content—and this often focuses on the three domains of self, others, and the world (recall from Chapter 3). Wholesale changes are not necessarily common, though they do happen. More likely, your clients will make some degree of alteration to their existing way of viewing the world that more closely aligns with their experiences.

Regarding beliefs about the self, perhaps your clients once viewed themselves as helpless or weak, and through suffering found new levels of empowerment and strength that they could not comprehend when the suffering began. Conversely, some clients may have held tightly to the need to control, and through their pain they have surrendered this desire and replaced it with mindful acceptance. Many people—both clients in therapy offices and research participants in studies of posttraumatic growth[47]—report being stronger or more resilient than they thought. It is your role to attend to these changes and help your clients connect these new beliefs to their sense of identity, while affirming the worth of their new identity. Joanna, for example, was unable to reconstruct an identity centered on loving her son until she was at a place of acceptance and had challenged her beliefs that no longer were adaptive.

Regarding beliefs about others, while suffering can cause clients to turn away from others or become anxious about the relationships they do have, existential reminders elicited by suffering may evoke a desire to improve their close relationships. Researchers have found that after being reminded of death, people were more likely to offer forgiveness to those with whom they had a close and committed relationship.[48] This positive effect of death comes from increases in empathy: When people think of dying, they begin to feel more empathic toward those who hurt them. A recent systematic review of seventy-three studies conducted over two decades revealed that when people are reminded of death, they become more committed to their close relationships, view their romantic partners more positively, and seek to be more intimate with their partner.[49] Suffering has a way of cutting through the relational drama that does not matter. Joanna was able to reform her views of what was important to her. Her priorities shifted to focus less on work and more on her connection with her son, her parents, and her close friends.

Regarding beliefs about the world, your clients may jettison a belief in a just world, no longer adhering to the notion that life is fair, that hard work pays off, and that people get what they deserve. Instead, they may acknowledge the randomness in life and attempt to find a deeper connection to nature or the cosmos. This was the case for Joanna. Through her experience, she discarded her belief in a just world and became more compassionate toward others who were struggling and started to envision a new identity where she might be able to help those who have survived medical traumas like hers.

Belief revision may also alter the *style* of beliefs. That is, your clients may change *how* they hold their beliefs, whether rigidly or flexibly. For some, facing existential concerns is deeply unsettling, and in the wake of groundlessness and anxiety, certainty can be appealing.[50] Those who have not fully processed or refuse to accept their suffering may look for an externally defined identity that seems to have all of the answers. As the pain lingers, some may seek out cults (or cult-like churches), defer to powerful authority figures, or become extremely dogmatic about their beliefs. However, doing so leaves clients in the same position as when their suffering began: They tightly grasp beliefs that are vulnerable to being shattered by future suffering when their beliefs do not hold up to the painful reality of life.

In our view, however, *adaptively flexible* beliefs may be better suited to withstand the storm of suffering. They bend but do not break. They provide security *and* permit growth and revision. For some clients, reconstruction involves shifting to hold more adaptively flexible ways of believing. This involves having some resolve and conviction in one's beliefs *and* also allowing for doubt, questioning, and a lack of certainty, which allows for future revision, if necessary.

Reconceptualizing Suffering

Often, you will need to help your clients reconceptualize their suffering in order to cope with it. This process can take different forms.

For instance, by helping your clients hold their pain *and* embrace the strengths that were demonstrated during their suffering, they may meaningfully re-narrate aspects of their experience. This can be done when your clients begin to reflect on how their suffering has changed them. Perhaps they have deepened their relationships, reprioritized their values, or shifted their sense of purpose. Joanna, for example, originally viewed her suffering only as a series of terrible losses: the loss of her dreams, the loss of her career ambitions, the loss of her son's future. However, by re-narrating her experience as one in which she demonstrated deep resolve and was able to find a more profound and complex love for her son in this process, she can both hold the pain of her suffering and see all of the ways her life has new meaning now. This does not disregard that her life was meaningful before her great suffering. However, it is a shift in that her life is also meaningful now, in a way that she did not expect. It's important to note that reconceptualization can only be done after you have walked the previous phases with a client. If you rush to reconceptualize your clients' suffering too quickly, your clients will experience this as invalidating and insincere.

You can also help your clients loosen or completely abandon some of their assumptions, such as the idea that "all pain is bad." You can help them come to understand that a meaningful life is full of pain and enjoyment, sorrow and joy, creation and loss, and that it is unrealistic to expect only to experience positive outcomes or to never feel pain. Helping point out situations of "both/and" in your clients' lives, and having them reflect on these experiences, can help jostle some of these embedded assumptions. Joanna found great meaning in her career, was devastated that it was snatched from her, *and* her life also has meaning now, even if it is in a way that she would never willingly choose.

Weakening the Myth of Greater Meaning

Roy Baumeister has argued that many people hold a myth of greater meaning,[51] which has two main components: completeness and consistency. The former suggests that absolutely everything should make sense, and the latter suggests that things should remain relatively static, constant, and permanent. It is the desire for coherence run amok. Baumeister and colleagues suggest that the result of the myth of greater meaning is that people expect their experiences to be persistently and pervasively positive and for themselves to be consistently fulfilled.

If everything should make sense, and if things in this world should be constant and unchanging, and life should be full of positive, feel good moments, then any kind of suffering can be devastating. While some who follow this myth may arrive at a more balanced view (e.g., some things make sense, but I can't explain *everything*), others may become nihilistic (e.g., everything in life is a fabricated illusion lacking inherent meaningfulness). Although there might be a short-term adaptive function in the nihilistic approach, in the long term, people will need a sense of meaning to thrive. That's why a more balanced, weakened view of the myth of greater meaning is a signal of adaptive, mature coping that is honest and genuine about the pain in life and one's experience of suffering.

Because this myth is so deeply engrained in so many people's cultural narratives (especially Western ideologies), you may have to help your client weaken this myth by asking, "Imagine what your life might look like if you didn't have to make sense of everything that happened. Instead, you could agree that some things may simply happen, and we'll never know why." This might provide some clients with relief as they explore the idea that they are no longer bound to work tirelessly to have everything make sense; they can embrace, rather than resist, change when it occurs; they might be more open to see the good within the painful.

For some, a different approach may be needed. You could help your client by asking, "Sometimes when we hold onto things tightly, it can be because we are afraid or threatened. Can you identify the threat that you feel?" Help your client reflect on this and then ask, "Often when we experience fear, we are trying to protect something that we love. Can you identify what you love that you are afraid of losing?" This will help your clients understand their hesitation of revising this myth and begin the process of untangling their fears from the existential reality that suffering exposes. For example, Heather felt anxious and fearful after she had deconstructed her belief about God's protection; she did not know how to make sense of her life after doubting this fundamental belief she had held for so long. By highlighting in our sessions that we don't always have to make sense of everything, Heather was able to hold in tension a belief in a God she loves, even when she cannot make perfect sense of how this God may be relating to her. By helping her see that she can *both* believe in a God *and* not fully understand how this God works, she was able to reconstruct a new way of understanding and relating to God that was authentic with her experiences. Addressing the myth of greater meaning can help facilitate the healing process of *both/and* thinking. (We provide an example of this in the application section that follows.)

In this reconstruction process, you can help your client realize that some suffering cannot be neatly explained or reasoned away. Given our human desire for coherence as innate meaning-makers, one way to make sense of suffering is to acknowledge that some suffering is simply senseless. Ironically, this interpretation can fit into a coherent worldview, in which one does not demand that everything makes sense.

One of the strongest contributions of suffering to a flourishing life may be the freedom that comes from weakening the myth of greater meaning. People can honestly look at existential realities that frame human life and not view them as threats that need to be defended, but rather as truths that need to be embraced. Then, they can respond with authenticity and intentionality, as they seek to live meaningfully in each moment, not because life owes them meaning, but because they choose to create it.

Placing Suffering in the Context of a Narrative

Narrative theory assumes that everyone tells stories about their lives, which helps them make sense of and derive meaning from their experiences.[52] But two problems may arise when clients try to fit their suffering into their life story. They may avoid or deny their suffering, failing to acknowledge its rightful place in affecting their life. Alternatively, they may have a narrative that focuses solely on their suffering, thereby defining themselves only by their adversity. Narrative therapy helps clients position their suffering in its rightful place in their life story—present but not exclusively defining—so they can see, and construct, a richer and more complete view of their life.[53]

People often view their suffering as a major signpost in the story of their life, bifurcating time into segments: before suffering and the period after. There are advantages and disadvantages to this approach. In one sense, it's quite helpful to see the positive ways that one's perspective has shifted. People's beliefs, particularly about suffering, are different, and they may embrace existential realities as facts of life. So, in a real sense, they *feel* very different.

However, out of this false dichotomy, some clients become too attached to how they used to see the world; their old beliefs persist. They long for the naïve innocence that was lost in their suffering. Others grieve the actual losses of life, health, or dreams that can never be reclaimed. They cannot accept the reality of their life or their new sense of identity. Still others derogate their "previous" self: They cannot understand how they ever held such ideals, why they foolishly believed what they did, or why they acted as they did. They split their life story into two distinct parts.

A more cohesive view, however, is that life is like a story that builds on itself. Each chapter contributes to the larger narrative, and every experience has helped shape your client's sense of identity. Instead of dividing their lives into the categories "before" and "after" suffering, it is more holistic and adaptive to help your clients think about how this struggle has played a vital role in shaping their identity. For example, Joanna originally viewed her story as having two distinct parts: before the traumatic birth of her son, and after. She viewed herself as competent, strong, and in control before her suffering. Since that time, she has viewed herself as dependent, fragile, and vulnerable. She sees her situation as something that robbed her of who she once was and dramatically altered her life story. Asking her, "Now that you have come to terms with your and your son's medical conditions, how do you see yourself moving forward?" can help start the process of casting a new identity. In addition, asking her, "What do you hope for when thinking about the future?" will help her begin to craft a narrative that is not solely defined by her past struggles. Finally, when she describes an identity and life that is more whole, you can affirm this and point out, "It sounds like you hope for a life that honors but is not solely defined by your suffering." As a broad, overarching, and evolving narrative, your clients' sense of identity consists of all of their experiences—including the ones that they wished were different.

(Former) Beliefs May Persist

Reconstruction is powerful, but it is difficult; not everyone is fully ready for this process. Because people see the world a certain way, they may readily fall back into previous ways of interpreting their experiences. Like grooves in a record, when the needle gets just a bit too close, it may easily slip back into the familiar pattern of comfortable, worn beliefs. This is especially true when your client is overwhelmed, stressed, or otherwise mentally taxed. People's default pattern of thinking will take over unless they are consciously and effortfully trying to override these deeply embedded ways of thinking. Over time, the pathways toward new beliefs will become strengthened with use, but in the beginning, and when stress is present, the inertia toward old beliefs will be powerful.

Some research illuminates how powerfully resistant beliefs can be. In two large cross-cultural research studies, researchers compared religious individuals (i.e., those currently identifying as religious), formerly religious individuals (i.e., those who "left the faith"), and never religious individuals (i.e., those who never identified as religious).[54] We might assume that once someone embraces a new identity, such as "not religious," their beliefs and experiences should more closely match others with the same identity. However, the results were revealing. On a number of different dimensions, formerly religious individuals demonstrated a pattern that was somewhere between currently religious and never religious individuals. Although they identified with other irreligious people, there was a *religious residue* effect: Once someone has been religious, the beliefs are so deeply engrained in their cognitive and emotional processes, that they persist, even after one's identity shifts. Even in active revision, old beliefs will continue to exert effects on your clients.

It is important for you and your client to be aware that the remnants of beliefs can have powerful effects. Your clients may feel frustrated when they easily slip into their old ways of seeing the world. They may be unaware that their deconstructed beliefs are still relatively intact and are guiding their thoughts and behavior. Joanna's belief in a just world slowly crept back into her parenting of her child who has special medical needs. She took meticulous notes of every doctor's appointment and fastidiously adhered to every medical recommendation. She sought to exert control in a groundless world. However, her child still had unforeseen setbacks, and, in some areas, did not progress as well as predicted. Joanna expressed frustration that, given all of her hard work and investment and copious adherence to the stringent medical treatment plan, her child wasn't doing as well as she wanted. Her belief that this scenario was unfair was hard to shake. Encourage your clients that this process takes time, and it is iterative: They may have to revise, and revise, and then revise again, staying committed to the process along the way.

APPLICATION

For some clients, deconstruction and reconstruction may occur in tandem. As they question or remove beliefs, these clients may quickly replace them with new ones. For other clients, a period of complete deconstruction may be followed by a distinct phase of rebuilding and reconstruction. Because of this variation, it is important to avoid clinical rigidity and stay attuned to each client's natural process.

Modeling Openness, Curiosity, and Grace

Do not expect perfection, or even consistency, in the new system beliefs that your clients reconstruct for themselves. Some new beliefs resonate immediately; others are honed and developed over time. Flourishing requires that people continually evaluate their beliefs and revise their way of interacting with the world based on their experiences. Reinforce in your clients that failure is permissible and is indicative of a learning, growth-focused mindset. Your clients should not demand perfection from themselves. Rather, they should embrace openness to new ideas, explore curiously, and learn to give themselves grace.

To promote this practice of openness, curiosity, and grace, carefully attend to your own language and be intentional when communicating. Guard against statements such as "things are now better" or "now that the pain is behind you." Because the pain of their suffering has shaped and been incorporated into their new identity, it is important not to create false dichotomies between "then" and "now." Also, insist on honesty. Your client may see you as someone whose beliefs are solidified and who has life figured out. Do not pretend this illusion is accurate. Instead, walk this process with them, knowing that being honest will elicit honesty from them.

Finally, never talk down to your client. When they fall back into old patterns of thinking or avoiding, kindly prompt them back toward the task of rebuilding their identity by reshaping their beliefs. Your constant commitment to their progress will serve as an encouragement when their motivation wanes.

OPEN POSTURE PRACTICE. A practical application of promoting openness is through the open posture practice. The goal of this practice is to help your client surrender control and accept their new identity. Have your client sit with their feet flat on the floor and their hands resting palms-up on their legs. With their eyes either opened or closed, have them repeat "yes, yes, yes—I accept who I am in this moment." This physical act of an open posture, along with the verbal affirmation, reinforces their sense of autonomy in choosing their acceptance of their new identity. It removes their defensiveness about how they want or think the world should be, teaching them to actively accept, rather than fight, reality.

Provide Space for Active Reconstruction

To start the process of reconceptualizing suffering, help your clients understand that changing their beliefs corresponds with changing their identity, because how they see the world is related to how they see themselves. Once they understand this important connection, you can help them identify which beliefs match their new experiences and new identity. Give them the opportunity to reflect on how their suffering has changed what they believe and how they see themselves, and provide them space to clearly articulate some of the new beliefs they hold in the wake of their suffering.

MOTIVATIONAL INTERVIEWING. Following deconstruction, your clients may feel ambivalent and uncertain. A way to help them move from a state of feeling stuck or groundless to an active state of reconstruction is though motivational interviewing. Motivational interviewing, a therapeutic technique that helps people move toward greater activity and flourishing, helps people clarify their values and priorities by asking them who they want to be, where they want to be, and what they want to have in the future.[55] The process of reconstruction is where people build up new beliefs that are aligned with their view of the world in the midst of hardships. Once your clients have accepted their reality (e.g., my loved one has died; we will not have children), they begin to envision their future accordingly, and start constructing their daily lives in ways that build purpose to meet these goals. You could ask your client, "If what you believe now is really true, how does this new belief change and inform your life?" In other cases, such as that of Matthew, an exchange could go like this:

Therapist: Matthew, what do you imagine your life looking like now? What do you hope for the future?

Matthew: Well, I want to live a full life.

Therapist: What do you imagine that looking like?

Matthew: I hope that I could cope with my Bipolar disorder.

Therapist: What would that look like?

Matthew: I wouldn't have it ruin my life. I'd be able to finish college, hold down a good job that would cover my bills, and I could help others. That'd be a full life.

This technique allows you to use the information clients share to clarify how they would like to orient their behavior to form an identity that is in line with the full reality of their suffering. This helps your clients engage in autonomous identity formation, paving the way for the next phase. As you shift their new beliefs from theoretical to practical, you are helping them put their beliefs into practice in tangible ways. This helps build coherence by organizing a life that makes sense and is centered around a genuine reality. It can make people feel as though they matter and can help them regain a sense of purpose that is aligned with broader goals that are congruent with their newly envisioned future.

USE "BOTH/AND" LANGUAGE. Some clients may ignore or dismiss their suffering as being "in the past." They might also say it no longer affects them. Other clients may disparage their "previous self" as immature or foolish. Still others will long for the life they led prior to their struggles. This view can impede the reconstruction process of forging a coherent narrative. One way to help your clients tangibly see the powerful effects of integrated living is through using "both/and" language. As your clients describe their experiences, carefully attend to their language. The use of "but" or "or" naturally creates a comparison that can contain value statements. For example, your client might say, "I wanted to be a parent, *but* now I never can." This suggests a bifurcation in identity, implying a natural judgment. Instead, help them reframe that as, "They wanted to be parents, *and* now they are living a childless life." An exchange with a client like Joanna might look like the following:

Joanna: My life used to be on track, but now I feel like everything is in ruins.

Therapist: Tell me what you mean.

Joanna: Before Harold's birth, I had things together. Really. My life was going places. And I had a handle on things—my career, my friends, my own desire to be a mother.

Therapist: And now?

Joanna: Now? Everything has changed. I mean, I don't believe that life is fair anymore. And I certainly don't believe I have control. I gave up on that.

Therapist: It sounds like you look at your life in two parts: before and after Harold's birth.

Joanna: I guess so.

Therapist: I would encourage you to think about your story as, in fact, an unfolding story. Your life was going as you had hoped and planned, until it did not. This is a new chapter of your story; not the beginning and not the end. Your story is in process—as all of our stories are. Your beliefs of control were adaptive for you in the first part of your story, and now you have realized some new truths: You do not have control of everything. You are finding your son the best doctors and taking him to his appointments, which are areas that you do have control over, and at the same time you also don't have control over how he will respond to treatment. Both are true to your experience. You have control over some things and others you do not. It is "both/and."

A metaphor can often be helpful to your client in times like this. When we drive, we buckle our seat belts, look both ways before crossing an intersection, come to a full stop at a stop sign, and go the speed limit. However, we cannot control other drivers on the road. We can do everything as planned, and follow all the rules in our control, and yet we still do not have full control over what happens to us. Does this mean that we don't buckle our seat belt? No. Does this mean we don't drive? Absolutely not. But it does mean we learn to live in the tension of "both/and." We *both* buckle our seat belt *and* live in the full reality that we do not have full control of every outcome.

Encourage Identity Formation

Reconstruction leads to identity re-formation. Remember: Only your clients can determine their identity. It is their story to tell. They are exercising autonomy by rebuilding their beliefs and view of self. Your role is to increase their insight and help them make connections between their shifting beliefs and their new identity. You can help them understand that part of their identity includes their suffering. Your client does not need to craft a narrative in which they "defeat" their suffering. Rather, they must honestly acknowledge the role that suffering has played in their life, and how their identity has shifted because of it. At the same time, caution them that they should not be solely defined by their suffering—it should be part of their story, not their whole story. The latter is more adaptive and permits space for flourishing and growth. Moreover, as your clients adopt new beliefs, encourage them to find new ways to live out their purpose. For some, this might be generating new goals or aspirations. Although some purposes may be lost in suffering, new ways to find purpose may emerge that align with their new identity.

HAVE YOUR CLIENTS WRITE DOWN THEIR STORY. Writing one's story is a powerful exercise that can help your clients make sense of their experiences and craft a coherent narrative. Have your clients write their story, including their thoughts, feelings, and sense of identity, before, during, and after their active suffering. This exercise could be assigned as therapeutic homework that your client reads to you in a session. Look for ways in which their beliefs and perceived identity have shifted from before the suffering began to now. Similarly, look for consistencies and ways in which their identity has remained constant. As they reflect on their story and clarify their identity, they may begin to see meaning emerge. Moreover, they may realize that they had previously endured difficulties in the past, and their journey in suffering began far earlier than their original acknowledgement. In addition, they may see patterns of adaptive (e.g., continued resilience in the face of struggle) or maladaptive (e.g., avoidance or denial) patterns of dealing with pain. These processes can be addressed in your office, as your clients contemplate their new sense of self in light of their suffering.

INTEGRATING "SENSE OF SELF" MEDITATION. Once your clients have written down their story and you have processed that intervention with them during your sessions, you can lead them in a guided meditation. Have your client practice a meditative posture: finding a resting position, closing their eyes if they feel comfortable, and beginning to notice their breath. Have them reflect on a time when they were afraid while actively suffering (e.g., at the time of diagnosis, while their loved one was dying) and to observe their own face at that time. Have them recognize what was happening within themselves (i.e., what they were feeling in their body). Then, ask them to imagine bringing their current self into this meditation to meet their suffering self in that moment of fear. Invite the client's present self to give their suffering self some comfort, wisdom, or knowledge that the suffering self needs in that moment. It may be a hug, a kind look, or a word of wisdom or encouragement. Allow your client to sit in that moment. Have them touch their chest, thigh, or stomach with moderate pressure as they continue to notice their breath. Invite your client to bring their suffering self into this present moment, where they are now: with the knowledge of the pain of the suffering self and the wisdom and compassion of their present self. And just as the hand pressing on their chest is giving love to themselves, their chest returning pressure sends love back to their hand. They carry the love and wisdom with them and will bring their younger suffering self with them as they go forward, so they are never alone. Finally, invite your client to take three breaths in and out, and when they are ready, they can open their eyes.[56] After your client reopens their eyes, you can invite them to process what they experienced and learned.

REFLECTIVE MEANING-MAKING. This technique, which is equal parts educational and clinical, has your clients write out a mock obituary stating exactly how they want to be remembered. What things do they wish people will recall about the way they lived their life? How do they wish to be memorialized? This task, and other reflective meaning-making exercises, help move your clients to a level of abstraction where they are less caught up in their current distress and are more oriented toward a broader perspective. Priorities clarify in the midst of reminders of death and finitude. As they think about how they wish to be remembered one day, you can have them list concrete ways they can work toward these goals now. If they desire to be remembered as generous, what are they doing now to accomplish this goal? If they wish to be memorialized as a good friend, how are they engaging close friends and loved ones now? It is a helpful way to solidify one's identity and clarify one's priorities and purpose.

SUMMARY

As your clients reconstruct their beliefs, they will be forming a new identity, shaped in part by their pain and suffering. This is a major step for your clients in exercising autonomy, and you will be guiding them in this process, encouraging them to find meaning in their new identity. They will learn to link their beliefs with their identity, as their new beliefs shape their identity formation. You will help model openness, curiosity, and grace, as this process can be iterative and can involve continual refining. Over time, their new identity will materialize, and they will begin to emerge from the darkness.

7

Daylight:
Living Authentically

"I don't want to be swallowed by the darkness. Nor do I want
to be blinded by the beautiful facade. No, I want to be part of
a people who see the darkness, know it's real, and then, then,
then, *light a candle anyway*."
—SARAH BESSEY, *Out of Sorts*

LIFE IS FULL of sharp reminders of suffering. Even after the hard
work of deconstructing and reconstructing beliefs, and shaping a
new identity, reminders will bring back grief, re-open old wounds,
and plunge people back into familiar pain. We wrote the first draft of
this chapter exactly eight years after Tim passed away.

In the very same hospital, in the very same waiting room, we were
in for Tim's surgery.

Again, we were awaiting the outcome of another heart surgery:
This time, it was for Daryl's dad.

This nearly identical surgery to the one that claimed Tim's life
brought many of the same memories, emotions, and thoughts
back. Tim's death prompted his dad to undergo medical tests, which
revealed that he, too, needed heart surgery. Four years ago, that
surgery spared his dad's life. Although he had recovered well, an
unexpected problem developed, which required a higher risk and
much more complicated surgery. We booked a flight to ensure Daryl
could be there with his mom during this second surgery. The entire

situation felt like a recurring nightmare that brought on the all too familiar pangs of fear, grief, loss, and helplessness.

And in other ways, we were not the same as we were eight years ago. We'd discarded many beliefs we used to have that did not hold up. Our spiritual views had changed (and deepened). We no longer only expected positive outcomes or believed in a fair or just world. We had worked at deepening our intentionality with each other. We are not perfect, nor have we solved these existential quandaries; rather, we continue to learn to live with the constant knowledge of them and have come to accept these existential concerns as facts and not fears. Through this, we have some practice facing our pain and fighting the urges of experiential avoidance, and we have developed a few ways of engaging our suffering.

Daryl's dad emerged from this incredibly difficult heart surgery with what seemed like miraculous success. We were relieved. We celebrated. It felt like this time *was different*. Finally, life was settling out, and things seemed hopeful again.

Then, six days after surgery, Daryl's dad showed a significant complication that resulted in a serious brain bleed. As he was in and out of a medically induced coma and countless intensive care units, every feeling of grief, sadness, injustice, anger, fear, and confusion came flooding back. Six days turned into six months, and over those next six months, we experienced the extreme highs of hoping for a recovery, and the crushing lows of realizing he never would. Each day gave way to new pain, as he slowly slipped closer to death, and we came to terms with the reality that this genetic disorder would claim another life. After six anguishing and discouraging months, Daryl's dad died. Fresh suffering stung anew.

Like us, your clients will emerge from a period of reconstruction to face a "new normal": a revised identity that has remnants of the old self and manifestations of a new life. They are the same people, but their identities and realities have evolved. They have the strength of surviving some of their most unimaginable fears—and continuing to choose to flourish even in the wake of those fears.

Authenticity

If suffering is like being in the darkness, eventually your clients will reemerge and adjust to the light of day. They will start the process of living into their "new normal" and may report that they *feel* like they are no longer actively suffering. However, suffering leaves scars, and your clients will have to bear them as they encounter reminders of their pain. Coming into the *daylight* means choosing to live authentically, striving toward building existential security and resilience, and cultivating vulnerable compassion with the lessons learned in the darkness.

THERAPEUTIC APPROACH

In this "final" (defined) phase of light, the central therapeutic goal is to help your clients achieve a sense of *authenticity*. In our view, an authentic life is a meaningful life: one marked by coherence, significance, and purpose amid suffering. There are three components to helping your clients develop an authentic sense of self: (a) helping your client align their behaviors and life with their new beliefs; (b) building existential resilience, where your clients view existential concerns as truths and not threats; and (c) promoting your clients' cultivation of vulnerable compassion. Reconstruction focuses on your clients rebuilding and revising their beliefs (i.e., cognitions); daylight, in contrast, involves supporting them as they bring their behaviors in harmony with these new beliefs in an authentic and genuine way, which will provide their life with a deep and robust sense of meaning.

However, when future suffering reemerges, some of your clients may feel the urge to once again respond with avoidance. Avoiding pain is deeply etched into the way that most of us live our lives, and at times it may even have been protective. In this phase, you can help support your clients to make the choice to hold on to what they have learned and commit to living authentically, rather than slipping back into older patterns of avoidance. Doing so helps prepare your clients for future periods of darkness ahead.

DESCRIPTION AND RESEARCH
How Does Suffering Change People?

Before we take a look at the components of an authentic sense of self, it is important to take a step back and examine how working through the phases of darkness might change your clients. In the wake of suffering, people report feeling different. Many express experiences of *posttraumatic growth*, which is the phenomenon where, following adversity, people tend to report positive changes in their life, often facilitated by finding meaning.[57] Many people are motivated to perceive that they have grown.[58] The research on posttraumatic growth has burgeoned, but there is some debate as to whether people have actually changed *because* of adversity, or if they somewhat put down their pre-trauma selves,[59] which is possible because most researchers ask people about their trauma after it occurs.[60] Because memory is biased and people may want to believe that suffering has created growth, it is hard to determine if they have *actually* experienced growth. In addition, actual and perceived growth may be rather different.[61] In short, the research on posttraumatic growth is mixed and we don't yet know enough about this area to make firm, conclusive statements. However, various data suggest that some people do, in fact, experience positive changes.

Because research is still in the early stages of parsing this out, we suggest that you don't focus on whether or not your clients are now "better off" than before—that is an impossible question to answer because life doesn't afford people a "control group" where clients can compare their experiences of a life lived without struggles to their life lived with struggles to determine which would be better. Rather, we suggest you focus on helping your client live authentically and meaningfully, acting with intention, fully aware of the existential realities of life, and being genuinely compassionate toward the well-being of others by acting virtuously. These markers of the "good life" may be more valuable than growth, in part because growth is not guaranteed.

So, what changes might your clients see as they emerge into this phase of daylight? Notably, many of your clients will express that they have gained a different perspective.[62] That is, following suffering, coming to terms with existential truths, and becoming intimately acquainted with pain, your clients may gain a sense of wisdom. Features of wisdom include acknowledging life's uncertainty, developing a healthy balance between thoughts and feelings, and recognizing the limitations of being human. From our perspective, these are authentic and adaptive responses to existential concerns.

Your clients may also gain perspective in knowing that they were able to survive such a difficult time in their life. They may realize their own strength and grit, or deeper appreciation of spirituality. Others may learn that they can rely on the love and support of others.

And, if they have put in the hard work of deconstruction and reconstruction, your clients' worldview will have changed substantively through the process of suffering. This includes what they value and how they see themselves, others, and God (or the Divine), as well as beliefs regarding whether life is fair, or how they even define "fair." As a result, this authentic sense of self better prepares them for future struggles. In our view, the ability to make meaning—by finding a coherent worldview, a community that provides significance, and a larger purpose that directs their life—is the surest way to flourish because of *or* despite suffering.

- Joanna's revised beliefs and newly formed identity centered around making connections with those she loved. Because she was able to now tell her story of her son's birth as one of love, rather than loss of control, she sought to become closer with her friends and family. This helped her come to peace with her fear of groundlessness. Through therapy, she came to realize that after she shifted her identity from one primarily focused on her career to one that prioritized relationships, she wanted to dedicate time for weekly meals with loved ones and started reaching out more. This change helped address her concerns with identity. She also decided to take her extensive knowledge of the medical world, which she came to know well because of her suffering, to create a support group for other survivors of traumatic births. Doing so helped her become more comfortable with the existential reality of death. Although this did not justify her suffering or take the pain away, it allowed her to live out her new identity in authentic ways that connected her with others who also were going through similar experiences.
- Heather's reconstruction resulted in a full acknowledgment of her mortality, which led to a desire to live with intention (facing her fear of death directly). Through working in therapy, she started to explore how to live this out. She decided to fill her life with things that make what time she had left full and meaningful to her: She reconnected with friends and decided to make those relationships deep and genuine; she decided to plant a garden for pleasure, where she could cut flowers and give them to her neighbors; and she decided she wanted to forgive members of her family who could not understand how to interact with her since her diagnosis. All these actions helped address her

fear of isolation. In addition, her shifting view of God and newly revised spirituality prompted her to stop attending church and instead connect with God through nature. Because she is still in the process of wrestling with her varying identities (e.g., person with cancer, high school student, daughter, friend), she is learning to live with this ongoing tension.

- Matthew's revised beliefs seemed more subtle, but the effects on his narrative, sense of identity, and life were profound. He shifted his identity from considering himself as "mentally ill" to seeing himself as someone who is empathic, artistic, and cares deeply about the disadvantaged. His work in this phase helped reveal how to live out this new identity authentically. Using his own pain and struggles, and because he knew intimately what it was like to live life at the fringes, his work in therapy helped him identify that he was motivated to work with those who were "on the margins." He first began volunteering to teach art to adults with developmental disabilities; then, he got a job working with children with severe autism. He also committed to finish college. All of these decisions provided him with a deep sense of purpose. However, even in the midst of this daylight, where dark pangs of suffering seemed to be relegated to the past, residual reminders emerged. Another Bipolar episode occurred, triggering his initial urges to avoid the pain and escape through substance use, and priming previous memories of his old identity as a "sick patient" and the longing to be "normal." He continually works to hold on to the progress he has made and the new identity he has forged, even when life's circumstances make it challenging to do so. And so, he lives in the awareness and tension of realizing that life is still groundless, and yet still incredibly meaningful for him.

Everyone's path to daylight is unique; therefore, this phase will look different for each client. The goal is to equip you with the skills needed to craft a helpful approach tailored to your clients' needs based on your own clinical expertise. In this final phase of suffering, your role as a clinician is more supportive than active.

Helping Your Client Choose Authenticity over Avoidance

Recall that pain-avoidance is a default response for most people. Even after experiencing suffering, your clients may want to revert back to comfortable patterns of avoiding pain and numbing uncomfortable feelings. But just as these responses only exacerbated their suffering before, without conscious effort, your clients may slip back into wanting to run from future suffering, which will make the anguish worse. It is helpful to remind them of this basic truth, perhaps by saying:

> "Once you feel like your suffering is over, it is common to want life to go back to 'normal.' But remember, that although you've changed and grown in different ways, your old tendencies to avoid or numb pain will still be there. Pay attention to when you feel like you are falling into old patterns and remember the techniques we talked about for tolerating uncomfortable situations and emotions. We can practice those again, if you'd like."

So how can you help your clients choose to live authentically? The first step is to help your clients identify how to align their values and behaviors. Authenticity requires the self-understanding gained from your previous clinical work together, so your clients' behaviors flow from their values, and are selfless rather than selfish.[63] Authenticity requires that your clients take ownership and responsibility for their decisions, even when doing so is difficult or unflattering, and living in accordance with their values, even when they are not popular. They do not blame outside sources for suffering, but rather decide on how to live meaningfully in the midst of their pain. This "final" phase takes courage to uphold the clients' convictions in the face of judgment from others.

The work conducted in the previous phases of darkness helps your client build the self-awareness that is crucial for living an authentic life. (This is also why without pushing into the pain, honestly naming their suffering, and doing the hard work of deconstructing and reconstructing their beliefs, they may not ever achieve a sustainable sense of authenticity.) Now, they will need help navigating how to live out this new identity.

Helping your client live authentically means talking with them about their *intentions* and *behaviors* and identifying the anxiety that lives in the space between those two. For example, after changing many of her religious beliefs, Heather found that it was more authentic to stop attending church and began to cultivate a spirituality that was nourished by time in nature. This caused her parents to respond with anger and concern because they were worried that she was abandoning, rather than evolving, her faith.

Initially, Heather resisted making any changes in her church attendance for fear of how her parents would respond. Many people give into that anxiety and revert back to their old ways of doing things. However, you can help your clients see that this anxiety is because they have found a growth-edge—something that is uncomfortable because it is stretching them in healthy and adaptive ways—rather than the familiar anxiety of groundlessness they felt while in the darkness of suffering. Understanding this difference will help your clients begin to live with this growth-related anxiety. Pointing out to Heather that anxiety accompanies changes, especially regarding deep and important values such as religion, helped her make sense of her feelings of uneasiness. As your clients see the benefits of acting in ways that are authentic, the anxiety will decrease in intensity.

Over time, the feeling of congruence will far outweigh their residual anxiety, and they will become comfortable in this new way of living.

The Importance of Building Existential Resilience

Helping your clients achieve an authentic sense of self also involves encouraging them to integrate their past experiences in a way that will build a sense of resilience for future episodes of suffering. We introduce the idea of *existential resilience* by building and expanding upon previous research on *psychological resilience*, which describes people who are able to successfully adapt to negative life events by viewing them in a particular light, managing them in productive ways, and transforming them into positive experiences.[64] In the midst of suffering, people who are able to find meaning and make sense of their situation (even when that means accepting the idea that some suffering is simply senseless) may begin to demonstrate resilience. Research suggests that resilience is a protective factor following both adversity and stress across the life span: It can help facilitate adolescent development in the face of struggle and predicts the ability to "bounce back" among adults facing difficult situations.[65] For both adolescents like Heather and adults like Joanna, when people demonstrate resilience, they are able to experience flourishing again, and more quickly, following negative events. Because of this, helping your clients build resilience now should help them cope with suffering again in the future.

Building on previous research exploring resilient reintegration,[66] we suggest helping your clients form what we call *existential resilience*, which we define as the ability to find meaning, endure adversity, and experience existential security. The first two components are relatively straightforward: (a) Existential resilience is marked by establishing a coherent way of making sense of the world, discovering sustainable sources of significance, and achieving an enduring purpose that transcends oneself—all of which must be able to withstand future periods of suffering. In short, this feature of existential resilience is about finding meaning. In addition, when future existential concerns arise, (b) those with existential resilience are able to endure them with resolve and humility. They acknowledge existential concerns as truths and not threats; as facts and not fears. This requires a humble acceptance of the limitations of the human condition and a powerful resolve to face them squarely. Both humility and self-regulation help promote endurance in future periods of pain.

The third, and perhaps most central, feature of existential resilience is (c) the ability to maintain *existential security*. Existential security is a sense of resolution—however tentative—regarding core realities of existence and themes of suffering: groundlessness (control or freedom), isolation, identity, and death. It does not imply that your clients will be free from anxiety when confronted with these issues, nor does it suggest that your clients have completely solved these intractable problems of being human. Rather, it is the acceptance of their personal frailty, life's finality, and their smallness in the universe. Heather came to terms with the reality she was dying. She viewed her mortality as a fact, and rather than be paralyzed by this fear, she turned this into a motivation to live intentionally. Of course, the fear of death never fully subsided; she lived with this knowledge, and in the tension of this reality, every day. Yet she was able to make genuine connections with friends, family, and her neighbors, which made her life meaningful.

Existential security is more of a state than a trait. It exists in matters of degree, and can come and go (often in waves). Moreover, your clients can experience existential security that allows for pain, acknowledges the tension in their beliefs, permits doubts and questions, and concedes that their current way of resolving these concerns may be insufficient and could change. Existential security provides a sense of peace in the wake of this uncertainty.

Research suggests that when people have existential security, they should be less defensive and reactive to perceived "threats" or reminders of existential concerns.[67] For example, people typically have negative and defensive psychological reactions to reminders of death.[68] These responses include increased anxiety and dissociation, the latter of which can lead to PTSD-related symptoms. When people dissociated as they thought about the traumas that elicit existential concerns (e.g., natural disasters, terrorist attacks), they reported worsened mental health outcomes. However, those that did not dissociate—those that leaned into their adversity and faced their existential concerns—did not report greater anxiety or PTSD.

Existential security is also associated with greater openness to new experiences and tolerance of those who are different, whereas existential anxiety is associated with prejudice, anger, and negative interpersonal reactions.[69] Those who have existential security may feel comfortable enough to seek new experiences, new relationships, and new ideas. They have cultivated *adaptively flexible* beliefs (during reconstruction; see Chapter 6) and have the emotional resources to experience growth. This ability to link existential security with the potential for growth is a vital part of building existential resilience. Matthew had to come to terms with the reality that his Bipolar disorder would persist, and life was not predictable; he faced his fear of groundlessness with a resolve to enact change in the areas where he could. By finding some degree of existential security, he was able to experience growth by deciding to volunteer with children with autism.

EXISTENTIAL REALITIES AS TRUTHS NOT THREATS. So, just how do you help your client cultivate a sense of existential resilience? The hallmark of existential resilience is the ability to view existential realities as truths, not threats. The certainty of death, the potential for isolation, an individual's lack of control, unclear identities, and a lack of inherent meaning are all facts of life. However, these facts often elicit fear. The reminder of an impending death can nearly paralyze people. At the same time, facing existential anxiety can catalyze authentic living: When faced with reminders of life's frailty, people can decide to live intentionally and honestly. Researchers call this the "roar of the awakening," and it often happens when death or other existential concerns take center stage in someone's life.[70] You can build this into all of the phases, but in this phase, you are intentionally increasing the language of existential realities: Name them as truths, and then your clients will start to do the same. For example, you can say to your clients, "I have found that change in life is a constant (ground-lessness), death is a reality that we all must face (death), no one else can really understand our own individual lived experience (isolation), and we are always evolving (identity). These realities can make mean-ing feel elusive (meaninglessness)." As you increase the use of this language and dose it to fit what you think your client is ready for, you will find that as you highlight its emphasis and use, your clients will begin to mirror this same language and understanding. Soon, they will see these existential realities as true (and unsolvable) features of being human and being alive.

Tim was in the hospital for three weeks before he died. During that time, many potential futures were discussed in light of his fail-ing heart. One was living, long term, with an assistive device that would perform the essential feature of pumping blood. One nurse mentioned that a previous patient with this "heart pump" toted it in a backpack and bought a motorcycle promptly after checking out from the hospital. He had always wanted to ride a motorcycle and, with a new lease on life, decided to really, fully, live. People warned him that he might die. But he knew too well the reality of the human condition: We could *all* die at any moment, and he chose to make the most of the time he had in the way that was most authentic to him.

This is not to suggest that your clients will immediately take up motorcycle riding or engage in risky behaviors. Nor are we suggesting that acting flippantly toward death is necessarily healthy. However, your clients may decide to rid themselves of the emotional and mental "clutter" in their life, and live more *purposefully, intentionally, and meaningfully*. Research has identified how honestly engaging existential concerns, such as death, can lead to positive outcomes.[71] Some people may spend more time volunteering, donating their resources, or helping others. Others may develop a broader sense of tolerance or seek justice for the marginalized. Still others may start caring deeply about protecting and preserving the environment. Many clients may begin to prioritize caring for themselves by eating healthy, exercising, or going to annual doctors' visits or getting regular health screenings. Honestly confronting existential realities clarifies values and motivates people to live up to those values with purpose, like Matthew's work with children with autism.

For others, facing existential realities can help them realize the importance of their relationships. When time is limited or people feel isolated, they may seek to form, invest in, repair, or expand their close relationships. Some invest more in their community. They have fostered a deep appreciation for those who supported them during their suffering or have a better understanding of the value of a loving community. They have gained perspective, gratitude, and humility, and desire a greater unity for humanity, like Joanna starting a support group and Heather's new relational intentionality.

REMINDERS WILL RESURFACE. Existential resilience is important because reminders of suffering may regularly resurface. On the day Sara was transitioning out of a group practice and into her own clinical private practice—a dream she held for more than a decade—a package containing a baby's crib was delivered to our backdoor. Sara had been ordering the last few office supplies for her new space, and an error in the distribution center sent us a painful reminder of our infertility diagnosis on the day we were trying to celebrate a milestone achievement. It felt like a cruel joke or a twisted omen. She had ordered a storage basket and instead was sent a crib that we would never use. This was a tangible reminder that we will constantly face the challenge of our new reality, and that it is never easy to make the choice to face it rather than to run in the other direction. In the same way, Matthew's Bipolar episodes will continue, Joanna will have long lasting effects of her stroke and have to navigate her son's medical conditions, and Heather is still terminally ill. Suffering lingers, and it may never truly completely recede. And sometimes, the act of choosing to walk this path of suffering is, by itself, flourishing.

Cultivating Vulnerable Compassion

Another way to help your clients build authenticity, rather than avoidance, is by cultivating what we call *vulnerable compassion*. Many clients develop this after experiencing suffering; it describes how clients may use the depths of their pain to connect with others who are also suffering, transforming their suffering by connecting it to a larger purpose or cause. This compassion is vulnerable because it is born out of the reality of their own woundedness from suffering. This vulnerability also acknowledges the reality of existential concerns, and that their beliefs regarding these concerns are not certain and might be ever-changing. Moreover, their suffering has given them a depth with which to look at the world and those around them. This vulnerability turns into an authentic form of compassion toward others who are suffering, because they too know what it feels like to suffer. And those who have suffered can develop the courage to name and honor the suffering they see in others, rather than ignore it or try to explain it away. The courage to suffer in their own lives becomes the courage to help others in their darkest seasons of suffering.

Flourishing in the daylight phase is often about learning to live with the anxiety and sadness that your clients may experience every single day—and taking that anxiety and sadness to reach out toward other people and connect from that deep place of pain. In this way, vulnerable compassion often motivates clients to act virtuously, with care, service, justice, forgiveness, or sacrifice. Having known the pain of suffering, your clients may find purpose in helping validate the suffering that others around them feel.

APPLICATION

In this final season of suffering, your clients may feel as though their "active suffering" is in the rearview mirror. However, there is still some important clinical work to be done. With the central goal of developing meaning and authenticity, help your clients (a) find coherence by processing the ways that their life, although different, is still part of the larger narrative of their story; (b), cultivate significance by working with them to build existential resilience for future seasons of suffering, and; (c) develop purpose by encouraging the nurturing of vulnerable compassion. In the text that follows, we discuss some applications and useful practices.

Practicing Integration: Coherence

Your clients may need help aligning their behaviors with their new identity. Helping them reach congruence facilitates a sense of coherence (i.e., things make sense) and builds an authentic life. For some, shifting identities and behaviors can mean that certain communities are no longer encouraging. A church that was once supportive may now feel isolating and incongruent. A group of parents who were once close friends may become a searing reminder of loss. Your clients may need to find a support system of people who have felt the sting of suffering. This will sustain them as they work toward the integration of their identity. To help your clients bring their behaviors in harmony with their newly reconstructed beliefs and revised identity, you can help them identify some of their key motivations.

MOTIVATIONAL CHECKLIST. An important part of the integration process is to support clients by helping them hold onto a reason or maintain motivation to do this hard work by asking them what makes enduring the discomfort worth it to them. Why should they ask these difficult questions? For some, it may be to honor the memory of a deceased loved one. For others, it is to find peace in the midst of their anxiety. Have your clients write down their reasons. They can take a copy with them and use it as a reminder and a motivator for when the pain and uncertainty overwhelm them. They may want to put it someplace where they look every day (e.g., bathroom mirror, the background on their cell phone, dash of their car; some clients have even tattooed this on themselves symbolically) so they can focus their intention and effort on the reasons why they would continue to ask these questions, even as they feel uncomfortable.

In one session, Matthew's existential fear of groundlessness was running rampant. He was fearful his Bipolar disorder was overtaking the rest of his life again. He was considering dropping out of college and was experiencing suicidal ideation. In this case, it was helpful to find a motivation for Matthew to stay engaged in the process of facing his fear of groundlessness. Specifically, this motivation centered around him staying in college, with the goal of finishing his degree, so that he could work with people in the margins. He had already accepted the reality of his suffering, and he was living into his new identity, yet another season of suffering was upon him—his Bipolar disorder episode was recurring, and he felt out of control. It was necessary to help Matthew discover a reason to persist, even in the midst of the pain.

Matthew: This is just too hard. I don't really see the point. I can't go on.

Therapist: Matthew, this is very painful. It is really courageous that you named that.

Matthew: Yeah, thanks, but I'm still in pain. This really sucks.

Therapist: It really does. And it is not fair. I hear you. Tell me, Matthew, why do you still persist?

Matthew: What do you mean?

Therapist: Why did you get up today and come and see me?

Matthew: I want more for my life. I don't want to be captive to my Bipolar disorder.

Therapist: Matthew, I totally agree. Tell me, what do you want?

Matthew: Well, I want to graduate college.

Therapist: Tell me about why you want to graduate college.

Matthew: Because, I want to help people who are struggling, like me. It's so painful, and I don't want them to feel like I feel.

Therapist: That, right there—that's it. That's why you persist. That's what got you up this morning. That's what brought you here. And that's what you are faced with this very moment. That's what we hold onto when it gets painful like this.

During this session, Matthew also completed a safety contract, and in the section titled "A reason worth living is:" he wrote, "To help others." Although the loss of control elicited by another Bipolar episode reignited his fear of groundlessness, finding a reason to persist helped bring his behaviors in harmony with his values, even when it was difficult. Even after many sessions, this reason became a central motivator to stay engaged in the difficult work of living out his suffering when college became challenging, when relationships became difficult, or when his job was stressful. What kept him persisting (and alive) was helping him hold on to the meaning he wanted to make by improving the lives of others.

Building a Capacity for Existential Resilience: Significance

Future suffering is all but guaranteed. Because suffering entails confronting existential realities, the ultimate goal in all of your work with your clients is to build a capacity for existential resilience—the ability to wrestle with existential issues in ways that build meaning and promote flourishing, in large part by conveying a sense of significance. This is a mark of authenticity in the wake of suffering. We suggest several ways to cultivate this capacity.

Have your clients reflect on what they have learned in their suffering: How have they changed? Have they perceived any growth? In what areas have they simply survived, and in what areas have they thrived? What are the assumptions or beliefs they no longer hold? What has replaced those? Building a self-awareness related to their existential resolve, and potential existential growth, will equip them for future encounters with suffering. They will know their strengths and weaknesses, as well as what seems to work for them. Finding existential resilience will help them feel a deep sense of significance in the world.

GUIDED IMAGERY OF EXISTENTIAL CONCERNS. Building existential resilience can be facilitated by guided imagery. This can usually take place within a single session, though clients who are particularly unsettled by these concerns may require small bouts over several sessions. Before starting, it is important to explain to your clients what they are about to experience and offer them the opportunity for a full description before starting this exercise; because they are being directly exposed to their fear, this can be a difficult process, and you will want their verbal consent. You will have to rely on your own clinical judgment to determine if they are ready for this imagery exercise.

First, your clients identify which of the existential realities (i.e., lack of control, isolation, identity, death) is their primary concern at that moment. Have them picture an image in their mind that captures that fear. It may even be a moment in their past when they have experienced that fear. Ask them to close their eyes, be aware of their breath, and notice how their body responds. Remind them that, at any time, they can open their eyes; you are with them and will help them process their feelings. Invite your clients to imagine this reality by picturing that image in their mind: They are out of control, alone, don't know who they are, or are near death. Ask them to describe what they are experiencing across all five senses (e.g., what they see, what they feel on their skin or in their body, what they hear, what they smell, if there are any tastes). After some time of active imagery, some clients may find a slight sense of peace or resolve; others may need to process with you after this exercise is over. In either case, it is helpful to make connections about how it might look to experience a meaningful response in the midst of this existential reality: *peace* when they are out of control, *connection* when they are alone, *being known* with an uncertain identity, or *living fully* when they are dying. The goal is to gently orient your clients toward meaning in the face of their deepest fear. Have them reflect on their meaningful response and again for them to describe what they are experiencing across all five senses. When you feel that adequate time has passed on their reflection, invite them to engage in three deep breaths; when ready, they can open their eyes. Once they open their eyes, process what they experienced when they engaged meaningfully with their fear.

One client's deepest fear was isolation. Her anxiety was rampant at the thought of being alone. When you ask her to imagine being alone, she describes being totally deserted in a wasteland. She describes feeling empty in her stomach, seeing a canvas of white nothingness surrounding her. It feels windy on her chapped skin. You ask her how she might find connection in that place. After some resistance, your continued prompts lead her to say that connection would feel like connection with herself. She says that knowing herself better and enjoying her own company would reduce feelings of loneliness. She sees her face, which is peaceful. Although she is not smiling, she is also not upset. Moreover, she says that even in her isolation, she takes comfort in connecting with nature, no matter how barren and empty it feels. She describes in detail a yellow flower that she notices in the corner of the yard. When the imagery activity is over, you can process with your client how to build meaningful experiences to enhance that connection with herself: spending time in nature alone, journaling, learning photography, and traveling alone. In this, your client begins to see that in her deepest fear of isolation, she is not overcome—she can thrive and find meaning.

IDENTIFY A SYMBOL OF YOUR CLIENT'S EXISTENTIAL RESOLVE. Some clients might benefit from acts that symbolize their existential resolve, such as carrying a small token or symbol that reminds them of their strength, perceived growth, or new perspective. Some clients get tattoos or piercings. Other clients might benefit from planting a tree that reminds them of a lost loved one and of the nature of life to continually grow. These steps can be practiced in anticipation of future existential angst, providing an anchor for their strength and resilience and serving as a physical reminder of the cyclical nature of the seasons of suffering. One client found a small pebble that had been worn smooth by the water continually washing over it; she carried it in her pocket as a reminder of her resilience. Whenever she felt pain, touching that rock would be reinforcement of her strength and resolve. She was a rock that had been worn smooth by the waters of suffering. For us, a symbol of life continuing was a spring robin. They are the earliest signs of spring in Michigan, reminding us that new life does come even after the darkest winter.

Encourage the Development of Vulnerable Compassion: Purpose

One way that your clients may find purpose in the wake of suffering is through expressing vulnerable compassion, which can be transformational. Brené Brown argues that vulnerability helps spring forth several prosocial responses: empathy, courage, joy, and love.[72] When people are in touch with their deep pain and can honestly, and authentically, share this with others, they are likely to respond kindly, lovingly, and bravely. You can help your client develop a deeper vulnerable compassion in several ways.

IDENTIFY NEW PATHWAYS TO PURPOSE. Previously, your clients sought meaning in ways that their suffering has now made difficult or impossible. Some may never experience being fully physically able to play with their grandchild. Some may never know the accomplishment of graduating from college. Physical, mental, or relational losses can alter how people seek meaning in life. Therefore, they must identify new avenues that bring a sense of purpose that is better aligned with their new identities. This process requires creativity. intentionality, and the changing of long-ingrained patterns of seeking meaning.

Heather previously found purpose through the church—primarily, the service activities it offered and the ability to connect with others. Once she stopped attending church, she struggled to have a strong purpose. An exchange to help her identify new ways to facilitate purpose could look like this:

Heather: I've been feeling a bit lonelier lately.

Therapist: Tell me about that.

Heather: Well, I've stopped going to church, and I'm missing my connection with other people. But I'm really loving my garden.

Therapist: I'm so glad that you've found gardening. It sounds really fulfilling. Tell me about this lost connection you feel.

Heather: Well, I had so many friends at church and opportunities for service, and now I'm feeling a bit lonely and out of touch.

Therapist: What does it feel like for you to be lonely and out of touch?

Heather: I feel like no one notices me. It feels boring and sad.

Therapist: What does this sadness bring up for you?

Heather: I feel scared that no one knows me, and that I'm in this world alone.

Therapist: I imagine that thought and your experience is really scary. Tell me a bit more about your gardening.

Heather: When I'm gardening, I feel like I'm nurturing other living things.

Therapist: I'm wondering if your newfound place of connection—your garden—might be a place to transform your isolation and feelings of loneliness and sadness.

Heather: What do you mean?

Therapist: Through your whole process, you've become so familiar with feelings of isolation. Your cancer diagnosis and losing your church community are reminders of this isolation. They have caused you to face this fear as reality, and you know how painful it feels. And because you know this pain, is there a way to use this knowledge for connection, rather than loneliness? Do you think there are others who feel lonely, where you might find connection?

Heather: I never really thought about it that way. I don't really know some of my neighbors. One of them rarely gets out; I bet she must feel pretty lonely, too. I could give her some of the flowers I'm growing in my garden.

Therapist: That sounds like a good starting point.

Heather's fear was isolation, so she was more attuned to the loneliness of others. She started bringing over flowers to her neighbors, which gave her a new purpose.

Summary

In the final season of suffering, your goal is to help your clients live into authenticity. This requires helping them integrate their life, in which their new beliefs and identity are consistent with their behaviors and life decisions. Your goal is to help them to live into this reality fully, to experience flourishing, and to equip them for future suffering by building existential resilience. Finally, you can help them cultivate a sense of vulnerable compassion for others, in which their intimate understanding of pain and suffering can genuinely connect them to others who are also suffering. As they accept their new life, and practice integrating different parts of their story, they can cultivate a courageous sense of hope for the future.

8 ⚹

A Flourishing Life

"The bravest thing of all is always hope."
—Brave Saint Saturn, *Binary*

The centerpiece of a flourishing life is the development of existential resilience by cultivating sources of meaning that can withstand future suffering. What might provide such resilient meaning? A 2018 assessment of meaning in America that sampled more than 900 people across two studies lends some insight: namely, religion, relationships, and helping others were determined to be the top sources of meaning.[73]

Building on this work, we encourage you to consider your client's *head*, *heart*, and *hands*. Specifically, what your clients believe (e.g., religious beliefs), how they relate to others (e.g., relationships), and how they live their lives (e.g., virtues) contribute to a rich and meaningful life, marked by existential resilience. In the text that follows, we briefly review the current literature around each source of meaning and suggest ways to help your clients cultivate meaning and experience flourishing across each of these three areas.

THE HEAD: RELIGIOUS BELIEFS

Religion has long tried to address the problem of human suffering. From the Christian account of Job wrestling with God during sudden adversity, to Buddhism's focus on how the solution to suffering is nonattachment and following the Eightfold Path, religion appears to offer comfort (if not solutions) during times of suffering. However, while religion is a primary source of meaning for many, its role in a person's suffering is nuanced.

A study of 4,675 participants from religious and nonreligious colleges, as well as community members that were sampled online, reported how many stressful life events (e.g., death of a loved one, parental divorce) they had experienced and the degree to which they experienced religious or spiritual struggles. Results revealed that both religious and nonreligious people can experience spiritual struggles when life gets difficult, and greater religiousness did not protect against these struggles.[74] Rather, the specific beliefs people hold may be more crucial in predicting who struggles and who flourishes. This means that rather than getting caught up in whether a client is religious or not, it is more helpful to focus on the specific nuances of your client's beliefs.

Sometimes religion can be helpful. One study of 169 bereaved college students who had lost a significant other within the past year asked students to complete measures of meaning, coping, and adjustment. The results showed that early in the process (i.e., within the first four months), religious beliefs interfered with the ability to find meaning; however, in the long term, religion was associated with greater well-being.[75] As we have seen in previous chapters, your clients may question how God could allow their suffering to happen; but once clients wrestle with these initial violations, religious coping can facilitate meaning-making and is associated with better outcomes. These results highlight that religion is beneficial when people can *use their religious beliefs to cope and make meaning.*

How might this process occur? Researchers have theorized that when religious people can *reappraise* their suffering in terms of their religious beliefs, they may be able to transform their suffering in ways that enhance their religious connection and deepen their faith.[76] To facilitate this, you can help your clients identify how their (revised) religious beliefs may address the various existential themes of their suffering. It is important to attune to how religion may help your client (by addressing existential concerns) and how it may hurt your client (by forcing a rigid worldview or not allowing space for "negative" emotions such as sadness and anger).

Other times, religion hurts. Not only do your clients' specific religious beliefs have the potential to cause distress (e.g., my view of God no longer makes sense), but their religious community can also prove a source of pain. Sometimes your clients' friends may offer religious platitudes to help make sense of their suffering, but really are trying to find coherence because your client's suffering threatens their own view of the world. The community may become defensive when your clients begin to ask complex theological questions that their suffering has unearthed, resulting in subtle excommunication from their religious community, which increases their feelings of isolation and loss (this was the case with Heather and her church). Still, some churches may promote an emotional prosperity gospel that lauds joy and hope, while disregarding or discouraging lament, grief, and despair.

Navigating Your Client's Religious Changes

What are common religious and spiritual changes following suffering? Some clients will experience *religious and spiritual elaboration*: They report a deepening of their beliefs and religious growth, where their beliefs become richer, more complex, and increasingly more nuanced and inclusive of other religious practices. Some experience *spiritual surrender*, where they find the deepest comfort in releasing themselves from the pervasive need to explain their suffering, and, in turn, trust that God, or some other higher power, has a plan for their life that is outside of their awareness. Some clients *double down* on their religious beliefs and compensate for their suffering by bolstering their core beliefs.[77] Other clients *become less religious* by either deemphasizing the role of religion in their life or more strongly emphasizing other sources of comfort. For some, this can lead to *religious deconversion* or *deidentification*: Some no longer hold any supernatural beliefs or engage in any more religious activities, some no longer wish to be affiliated with religious individuals or particular institutions, and some discontinue all religious practices.[78] On the other hand, rather than "lose their religion," some clients "reclaim their religion" and *convert* or *reidentify*. Because the confrontation with existential realities often causes people to reprioritize according to their values and what brings them the most meaning, some people, for whom religion had lost importance, begin to value religion again and return to the faith they previously held. Finally, some *switch religions* to a new set of beliefs that better explains their experiences and feels more authentic or genuine. For example, some clients raised in a Western, Evangelical Christian tradition may find aspects of the beliefs system in which they were raised to be constricting and insufficiently descriptive. In turn, they may begin to practice Buddhist meditation and embrace a view of spirituality that appreciates the connection of all living things. All of these religious and spiritual changes have the potential to move your client closer to what is authentic to them, which can in turn lead to a life marked by existential resilience.

Specifically, to help your client gain insight into their religious beliefs and connect them with their existential themes of suffering, you can ask your clients:

- In what ways do their reconstructed views of God or the Sacred now address the lack of control suffering revealed? Do these views now accommodate the reality of groundlessness in life?
- In what ways do they feel more connected to God, the universe,

or others because of their suffering? How have their spiritual beliefs reduced their feelings of isolation?

- What role does religion or spirituality play in how they view themselves as a result of their suffering? How central are these beliefs in their identity?
- How do their religious or spiritual views address the certainty of death? In what ways can they draw peace and comfort?
- How are they embodying or practicing these beliefs in a way that feels authentic to where they are now?

Developing Existential Resilience in Religion

Religion is an important component of building existential resilience because such beliefs help people develop lasting ways of experiencing *coherence*. Extending our discussion from Chapter 7, characteristics of existentially resilient religion include being:

- **Reflective.** Some of your clients take their religious and spiritual beliefs as givens without being explicitly aware of them. You can work to increase their insight into these beliefs by reflecting back to them, in their own words, what they are expressing that they believe, both through their language and in their actions. By modeling how to be reflective, they can begin to carry this practice out on their own.
- **Open.** Religious and spiritual beliefs can change over time. Resilient religion is reconciled with reality: It is responsive to evidence and open to differing viewpoints. You can help them identify the benefits of remaining open (i.e., adopting a growth mind-set) to change and learn from their experiences, others, the universe, and God. A marker of openness (and ultimately, resilience) is not being afraid when beliefs once again are challenged or change.

- **Secure.** Existential resilience requires balancing the openness to new perspectives with the security of key beliefs. Changing one's mind constantly or being persuaded without thoughtful consideration can be just as limiting as holding one's opinion with iron-clad closed-mindedness. After having reconciled with the reality of their suffering, your clients can benefit from identifying a few core axioms (i.e., irreducible central beliefs that your clients hold with a relatively high degree of certainty after significant scrutiny and critical examination). Holding key beliefs, while being open to change other ones, provides a degree of security when future suffering occurs.

THE HEART: RELATIONSHIPS

Building existential resilience involves developing healthy, meaningful relationships. Psychological research confirms that relationships are considered a bedrock of meaning in life. The need to be accepted by others is so strong that when people feel rejected, meaning in life decreases: across four experiments sampling more than 600 participants, when researchers excluded participants in the laboratory by having people refuse to work with them or ostracizing them in a shared activity such as a game, rejected participants reported lower meaning in life.[79] It is likely that your clients may fear not only being rejected, but also being *known and rejected*. Thus, one of the surest ways to build meaning and existential resilience is to have your clients cultivate and maintain healthy, reciprocal relationships, beginning with the relationship that you cultivate with them in your office.

Relationships can help your clients overcome feelings of isolation through a process called *I-sharing*. I-sharing is when people have nearly identical phenomenological experiences: They feel the same emotions in response to an evocative movie or piece of art, laugh at the same silly or absurd joke, or experience grief, loss, or heartache in very similar ways.[80] Ideally, your clients will be able to find moments of I-sharing with their friends and family. However, for those who do not have people in their life to which they can turn, you can facilitate these experiences in your office by communicating empathy via affirmations, nonverbal mirroring, and appropriate therapist disclosure (without shifting the focus to yourself).

Although relationships can be a source of great joy, they can also be a source of profound pain. Jean-Paul Sartre's famous quote, "Hell is other people," attests to this. At times, other people may try to *fix* your clients by offering "solutions" to your clients' pain and suffering. Other people may also *invalidate* your clients' pain by minimizing their adversity, saying that they know exactly how your client feels because they had a comparable experience, or searching for a silver lining (e.g., "at least your father lived a long life" or "they are free from pain now"). Sometimes, others may *judge* how your clients handle their suffering, as they may not be happy with or approve of your clients' new beliefs or identity. Your clients may also lament the times when others were notably *absent* during their suffering. Still other times, people are the *cause* of your clients' suffering because the choices of people in your clients' life may be, at least partially, responsible for their pain.

Building Existential Resilience in Relationships

Existentially resilient relationships provide a clear and consistent source of meaning, primarily through *significance*. They help your clients know that they matter, are valued, and are loved. You can help your clients learn how to navigate the challenges of well-intentioned but ultimately unhelpful friends and relatives, and instead focus on cultivating healthy, resilient relationships. To help your clients build relationships that enhance existential resilience, we suggest you consider the *ABCDE* of resilient relationships. These relationships are:

- **Affirming:** Help them find people who support their identity in the wake of their suffering. It can be incredibly valuable that they feel supported in ways that align with how they now see themselves. This may require that your client seek new friendships and new ways of meeting people.

- **Belief-congruent:** Your clients benefit from the consensual validation of being around people who have similar values or share a similar worldview, as we discussed regarding religious and spiritual communities. Encourage them to seek out connections that are consonant with those new values.

- **Comforting:** Your clients will adjust much better when adversity strikes if the individuals in their life provide direct, tangible support while withholding judgment. Encourage your clients to think about whether they have people in their life who can sit with them as they grieve, hug them as they cry, and listen to them when they are afraid—these are the relationships you can encourage your clients to nurture into rich and lasting friendships.

- **Disclosing:** We suggest you encourage your clients to focus on developing at least one close relationship partner with whom they can share their thoughts, hopes, dreams, fears, anxieties, and uncertainties. A long history of research confirms that disclosure is powerfully predictive of better adjustment and can transform people's lives.[81] Moreover, when there is mutual disclosure, the relationship feels more balanced and interdependent, and your client will be less likely to feel pitied or like a victim.

- **Empathic:** Without empathy, the relationship quickly becomes imbalanced as the less empathic partner becomes overly self-focused and can only see their own side. Empathy, however, encourages seeing the other person's perspective and seeking to know their experience. It also inspires reciprocal empathy, which is important in promoting I-sharing experiences and conquering existential isolation. Encourage your clients to develop empathy in their relationships.

THE HANDS: CULTIVATING VIRTUES

Our default reactions to events and to other people is self-protective and self-serving. But virtues, when practiced, are transformative—they can help people overcome their natural egocentric inclinations. *Virtues* are behaviors wherein people regulate or control these impulses and instead act for the well-being of others, such as altruism, sacrifice, forgiveness, or humility.[82] Research has found that the practice of virtues, or prosocial behavior, is associated with greater meaning in life: Four studies sampling more than 1,000 participants in total revealed that virtues, such as engaging in helping behaviors (i.e., altruism) or writing letters of gratitude, enhanced perceptions of life's meaning.[83] Research has supported the link between prosocial behavior and meaning in life because acting virtuously increases people's feelings of self-worth: When people act virtuously, they feel more worthwhile.[84] Therefore, helping your client cultivate virtues is a valuable part of developing existential resilience.

There are at least three pathways by which virtues help make life meaningful. First, they serve a *relational function*. Nearly all virtues are inherently social.[85] Virtuous behavior can help form, maintain, and repair relationships, including via forgiveness. For example, in a six-month study of more than 100 couples, participants reported meaning in life at the beginning and end of the study and indicated every two weeks throughout the study their level of forgiveness of their partner following an emotional hurt.[86] Results indicated that consistently forgiving one's romantic partner predicted increases in meaning in life during those six months. Relationships are what gives life so much meaning, and forgiveness helps repair those relationships so they can once again provide meaning. In the same way, humility can benefit relationships. Research has found that when both partners in a relationship act humbly, they have lower stress and depression, and better relationship satisfaction and health indicators—even during periods of stressful transition or conflict.[87] Specifically, a longitudinal study of sixty-nine first time parents found that following the birth of their child, participants reported better mental health when *both* partners were humble; similarly, when discussing a source of conflict while they were in the research lab, ninety-three couples reported higher relationship satisfaction and improved physiological responses (i.e., lower blood pressure) when *both* partners were rated by the other as humble. Because of this, people want to be in, and maintain their relationship with, virtuous partners, such as those with high levels of humility. It was even found that people rate humble potential dating partners as more attractive than arrogant ones.[88] In addition, people are more likely to forgive partners who are humble. Further studies have shown that people are more committed to and satisfied with virtuous (humble) partners: When participants in a study felt like their partner was humble, they reported greater relationship satisfaction with that partner.[89] In short, acting virtuously can launch a cycle of improving relationships for the virtuous person and their partner.

Another way virtues provide meaning is through an *expansive* or *transcendent function*; they help people see beyond themselves to connect with something larger, which helps them feel as though they are significant and life is purposeful.[90] Take for example, the virtues of gratitude and patience. Being grateful for gifts or benefits that people receive shifts the focus from themselves in the immediate moment. By practicing gratitude, your clients broaden their perspective to consider the positive roles that other people, God, or fate have played in their lives. Similarly, patience can help your clients move beyond their own immediate desires, and instead, carefully consider and wait for a desired outcome.

Virtues can also provide meaning by serving a *motivational function*. They can orient your clients' lives around an intention or purpose. A prime example of a motivational virtue is hope. Because people have difficulty finding purpose while suffering—and even more have trouble extracting purpose *from* their suffering, if there is even any to find at all—motivational virtues, such as hope, can help restore a sense of meaning by organizing their lives around an intention or purpose that is not yet realized.

Expressions of Virtue in Suffering

Virtues are powerful responses to suffering and may also be cultivated *as a result* of suffering. For instance, one longitudinal study sampled more than 1,200 college students two months apart.[91] Of these students, 122 experienced a traumatic event during the course of the study. Researchers asked participants to report on their lifetime trauma exposure; prosocial behavior, such as daily helping and volunteering; and meaning in life. Results revealed that both lifetime trauma and experiencing a trauma during the two months of the study were associated with engaging in more prosocial behavior; the study also revealed that these behaviors helped people feel like their life was more meaningful. Critically, some of the prosocial behaviors the participants engaged in were precisely because of the trauma, such as volunteering in Mothers Against Drunk Driving as a result of having a loved one badly hurt by a drunk driver. In this way, virtues help transform the participants' suffering and contribute to existential resilience by offering clients a sense of *purpose*. It also connected them with other people who had similar experiences and may understand and validate their identity. Indeed, virtues (the hands) and relationships (the heart) are symbiotic, often connecting people together. The virtues described in the text that follows, though not exhaustive, are particularly relevant for your clients as they develop existential resilience to better cope with their trauma or suffering.

HUMILITY. Humility is expressed by an honest awareness of one's strengths and weaknesses, a lack of superiority, and a prosocial orientation focused on the well-being of others.[92] Humble behavior in relationships is marked by empathy and selflessness, and strongly considering the needs of others. Intellectual humility is the awareness that one's beliefs (including religious beliefs) have limitations, an openness to new ideas and critical feedback, and nondefensively expressing ideas in ways that are not arrogant or demeaning.[93] In the phases of darkness, intellectual humility is particularly valuable in the deconstruction-reconstruction process. Clients who honestly assess their beliefs, acknowledge their limitations, and are open to criticism are able to revise their beliefs to better reflect their new reality.

Previous work has identified a possible intervention designed to cultivate humility.[94] The acronym for this intervention is PROVE. Have your client:

- *Pick* an instance where they were not humble: This helps clients realize that they can be prone to acting pridefully or arrogantly and highlights the interpersonal damage that a lack of humility can cause to other people.
- *Remember* what role their own strengths and abilities have in the larger scope of life: This helps clients acknowledge both their strengths and weaknesses, putting them in proper perspective of what really matters.
- *Open* themselves up to new experiences and information: This helps clients receive feedback and remain teachable by highlighting how doing so can be beneficial for your clients.
- *Value* all other living things: This helps clients reduce their

self-focus, resist feeling overly important, and increase their appreciation and love that extends beyond themselves.

- *Examine* their own weaknesses and limitations in order to commit to a humble way of living: This helps clients identify barriers to living humbly and teaches them how to hold on to the important goal of a humble life despite future challenges.

FORGIVENESS. Forgiveness is when your clients replace the negative emotions they have toward someone who hurt them with positive, other-oriented emotions, such as love and compassion.[95] The key to forgiveness is empathy.[96] Forgiveness is not excusing or condoning, and justice can still be pursued, precisely because forgiveness acknowledges that a moral harm was committed by the transgressor. Put simply, the fact that forgiveness is even needed recognizes an injustice has occurred. It is an intrapersonal process that takes place within the victim, with or without reconciliation. In some cases, reconciliation (which is the active repair and restoration of the relationship) is not desirable, such as in situations of abuse. Forgiveness is especially valuable in repairing those relationships that your client highly values and where risk for future exploitation is low.[97]

Like humility, forgiveness can be cultivated. Ev Worthington, an international forgiveness expert, proposed a five-step model for forgiveness, called the REACH model.[98]

- First, have your clients *recall* their hurt. They should think about the specific details of what happened and how it made them feel. The more vivid their description, the better.
- Next, have them *empathize* with their offender. This can be very difficult. Ask them to imagine what their offender was thinking or feeling when they hurt your client. What was their offender's perspective? Can your client imagine that despite the pain that

their transgressor caused them, it is possible that their offender really was sincerely trying their best, or may have been under stress or strain? When clients can take the perspective of their offender, it helps them move past bitterness and anger toward grace and benevolence.

- Once they begin to feel empathy, your clients can offer the *altruistic* gift of forgiveness. Only your clients can grant their forgiveness, and it truly is a self-sacrificial gift. Some clients will tell their offenders in person that they forgive them. Others write a letter. For others, communicating that forgiveness is not safe nor wise, so some clients may write in a personal journal that they have forgiven, and they can reference that as a tangible symbol in the future.

- Your clients can then *commit* to forgiveness. It can be challenging to remain dedicated to the decision to forgive. Negative emotions sometimes need time to dissipate and positive emotions need to be cultivated again. You can have your clients sign a "forgiveness contract" that includes the date they decided to forgive their transgressor, so they can reference it for the final step.

- Finally, your clients then *hold on* to forgiveness when doubts arise. There will be times when your clients question whether they have (or should have) actually forgiven their transgressor. Maintaining that commitment during turbulent times or when questions prevail will help your clients complete the ongoing process of forgiving.

GRATITUDE. Gratitude is the positive appreciation one feels when receiving a benefit from another person or an outside entity.[99] It involves the client's recognition that someone (or some larger force, such as God or nature or good fortune) has done something, largely unearned, to improve their well-being.

Gratitude can be especially difficult to practice when suffering.

Your clients may ask, rightfully, "for what do I have to be grateful?" With a nonjudgmental approach, help your clients identify some things, however big or small, in their own lives for which they can be grateful without being disingenuous to the way they feel. Some of your clients may not be able to express gratitude for their current state of health or their life situation and may thus need your help to do so. However small the object of this practice is (a sunset, a warm cup of tea, or flowers along the highway), it is meaningful.

There are several helpful techniques to cultivate gratitude: making gratitude lists or journals that your clients complete every evening; spending five to ten minutes thinking or writing about things for which your clients are grateful; and writing a letter to a specific person and reading the letter to that individual.[100] Alternatively, clients may simply want to express thanks to someone who has improved their life. If such behavioral steps are too much for socially anxious or introverted clients, they may prefer to write small notes of gratitude to share when the time is appropriate.

PATIENCE. Patience is the proclivity to "wait calmly in the face of frustration, adversity, or suffering."[101] Patience is derived from the Latin "to suffer," and has been described as the willingness to bear or withstand adversity or hardship.[102] Patience helps your clients endure when it is hard to live with intention—which promotes a sense of purpose. So many important yet meaningful goals are difficult and complex and so require time and consistent effort to achieve.

One way to develop patience is to intentionally practice difficult tasks. For example, if your clients write in a journal, encourage them to use their non-dominant hand. Perhaps they start with three minutes of writing, before switching to their dominant hand. Over time, they can build to five, seven, ten, or fifteen minutes. As the task gets longer, they will cultivate patience in doing something difficult. Another possibility is for your clients to intentionally do something in which they have no proficiency, such as learning a new language, taking up painting or pottery, or learning to cook. Doing so will be good mental practice for future events in which they must work hard, wait, and endure.

HOPE. Rick Snyder, an expert on hope, defined it as having three components: setting clear goals, understanding how to reach those goals, and having the motivation and ability to reach those goals.[103] Even in the face of stress or adversity, individuals who express hope are able to maintain a clear vision of a future goal, envision the pathways to reach that goal, and work hard toward accomplishing it.

To help your clients develop hope, begin by exploring their intentions and ensuring that their goals or purpose align with their values. Once they have articulated a vision of what they hope for in their future, discuss how they will make this hope a reality (e.g., reach those goals). Similarly, the ways in which they work toward their goals should be aligned with their values. By doing so, this increases your clients' sense of agency during a time in which they might feel like many things are beyond their control. When future suffering threatens your clients' well-being, hope can anchor them in the belief that they will endure it and emerge with a better knowledge of the depths of their strength.

The Importance of Self-Regulation

It is important to note that a core component in most of these virtues is self-regulation, which is the ability to overcome natural, often egocentric impulses in order to accomplish a more desirable goal.[104] You can think of self-regulation as the soil that helps virtues grow. Two major components of self-regulation are monitoring one's behavior and developing the strength to carry out appropriate behaviors.[105]

Your clients will benefit from continued self-evaluation and the practice of tasks to build their strength and capacity.

Similar to building muscle, initial efforts to self-regulate are difficult: Each instance of regulation reduces one's immediate ability to regulate again.[106] Or, to put it more plainly, continually acting with new levels of virtue and restraint is exhausting, and it is difficult to maintain. However, over time and with continued use, your clients' capacity to act virtuously will improve. This also means that these virtues take time to develop, and you can show your clients grace and emphasize the importance of self-compassion when they don't get it right the first time. Not only can self-regulation help your clients act more virtuously, it can also help them overcome the inclination for experiential avoidance in the future. Because the first reaction of many of your clients is to run from the pain—either by avoiding it, denying it, or numbing it—self-regulation gives them the ability to overcome this impulse and allows them to face their suffering courageously.

SUMMARY

A flourishing life is not one without pain. We still wrestle with the uncertainty of Daryl's health, even as more family members now face the prospect of heart surgery due to the same genetic condition. We continue to negotiate our new identity without children, and it still stings, albeit less, when people ask, "Do you have any kids?" Our suffering has forced us to face the reality of the existential certainties of life and we have tried to live more authentically in response—deepening, and changing, our religious beliefs; investing in our relationships with people who love us; and trying to make a difference in the lives of others—and we do so rather imperfectly. In the end, we have learned to hold on to hope in the face of uncertainty. And just like your clients may say, we do not know if we are better off because of our suffering. We would wish it away if we could, but life does not give us a chance for an alternate experience. We can only acknowledge the intentional work we have done, the reality that we now face, and the surprising connections we have found in the midst of this struggle. And still, we carry great sadness and longing.

In the same way, you cannot predict what the future holds for your clients, nor can you prevent future pain. But you can help them cultivate a full and flourishing life no matter what they experience. You can be the guiding support that they need during this time. You can provide a healing space for your clients when they are terrified that life is not what they had expected by attending to their head by discussing their religious beliefs, their heart by helping them develop healthy and genuine relationships, and their hands by integrating virtues into their daily life. A meaningful life is a flourishing life, marked by the courage to suffer and the courage to flourish—regardless of what comes next.

Epilogue

SUFFERING MOVES in seasons. At times, adversity overwhelms, and pain dominates. At other times, struggles seem distant and the burden feels light. However, suffering changes people in indelible ways; for many, its lasting effects on their lives linger. It takes courage to face the pain, to accept the hard reality of life, and to choose to live a life full of meaning.

We continue to try to find our way forward in life, embracing an identity that we did not foresee. We still miss Tim. We still lament not being able to have children. We still have nagging worries about Daryl's health. We still feel the acute grief of losing Daryl's dad. We lament as family members begin to show signs of this same genetic condition. These profoundly painful losses and times of sharp grief have brought us face-to-face with the existential realities that all must address. We admit our lack of control in this life. We know how isolating the world can feel. We realize that identities can shift and may need to be revised. We know that death is a reality. And in this, we strive to find ways to cultivate meaning. We try to live intentionally, because we cannot control the future. We try to seek out meaningful relationships with people who also desire lasting and deep connections. We make every effort to live authentically, true to our identity that includes our pain. We try to make the most of each moment, knowing that life is short and that we all eventually will die.

Living with the knowledge of these existential realities can enrich life. Sometimes, these reminders are a *gift*. Even if unwanted, they are still a gift. They clarify what is important, shift focus to things that really matter, and encourage us to live with purpose. Of course, to live this way is deeply painful, *and* it is also powerfully motivating. It takes hard work to transform suffering into something more, while still honoring the pain it causes and the ways it has changed lives. We haven't "conquered" our suffering—no one really does. It is a part of life that comes, goes, and sometimes stays, and finding meaning along the way helps make it more bearable.

Meaning is both an existential issue and central component of a flourishing life. Our hope is that by bringing together insights from existential psychology and positive psychology, this book has provided you with a rich, multilayered perspective from which you can engage your clients who are suffering. We hope that you have seen the "light" and "dark" side of meaning and have begun to think differently about suffering and the ways to best support your clients in some of their hardest moments of life.

You also can develop the courage to suffer—to bear with your clients in crises that have shaken them to their core, upended their worlds, and caused them profound pain. And while supporting your clients, you may have begun to think deeply about existential realities that have raised anxiety or prompted you to challenge your beliefs. Through working with people who are suffering, we are called into direct confrontation with the uncertainties of life. We hope that you have taken this time to think hard about your assumptions, critically examining how you reconcile these existential facts of life. Perhaps in working with your clients, you have found your own life to be changed. We encourage you to make existential considerations a regular part of your clinical work and contemplating them a consistent practice in your life.

The story of suffering is never simple; rather, it is wrought with pain, loss, and questioning, as well as with courage, growth, and intentionality. It is not something to triumph over, but rather an inescapable part of life. We will all suffer. *How* we do so matters. And because we shall all face these existential certainties, we are reminded that life is a gift, and we are offered a choice of what to do with that gift. Mary Oliver poignantly describes this human experience in the concluding lines of *The Summer Day*:

> "Doesn't everything die at last, and too soon?
> Tell me, what is it you plan to do
> with your one wild and precious life?"

Acknowledgments

WE WROTE THIS BOOK after our diagnosis of infertility, through the death of a parent, and amid marriage struggles. To say that we have all the answers would be inauthentic and untrue. Instead, we hope to share some of what we have learned, personally and professionally, to be true about suffering and how to embrace it as an inherent part of life—and how to find some way to flourish when life feels incredibly dark.

This book would not be possible without the support of others. We would like to thank the members of the 2017 Institute for the Research for Psychology and Spirituality (IRPS) for their helpful feedback regarding early phases of this project, including: Andrew Cuthbert, Ward Davis, Cynthia Eriksson, Julie Exline, Frank Fincham, Nick Gibson, Tyler Greenway, Liz Hall, Todd Hall, Sarah Schnitcker, and Everett Worthington. Specifically, we offer a special thanks to Don Davis and Joshua Hook for their continued support of our writing, their friendship, and for sharing this journey with us along the way.

We are grateful to our psychotherapists for their thoughtful and gracious wisdom as they walked through these seasons of suffering with us. We also thank Ann McKnight and Lynn Stubbs for their helpful feedback on previous versions of chapters. Your encouragement and excitement for this project was a gift. We are grateful for your wisdom and friendship.

Thanks to our friends who expressed genuine interest in our book, and continued love and encouragement, over its long development. We promise to spend more time with you at the lake now that we're done writing.

Finally, we are grateful for the editorial support provided by Angelina Horst and our editor Susan Arellano and the team at Templeton Press; their unwavering belief in us and continued guidance at every step of the process was invaluable. This book is only possible because you saw it as important and entrusted us to share our perspective. We are deeply grateful.

Notes

1. Frankl, V. E. (1959). *Man's search for meaning*. New York, NY: Washington Square Press.
2. Yalom, I. (1980). *Existential psychotherapy*. New York, NY: Basic Books.
3. Seligman, M. E. P., & Csikszentmihalyi, M. (2000). Positive psychology: An introduction. *American Psychologist, 55*, 5–14.
4. Wong, P. T. P. (2009). Positive existential psychology. In S. Lopez (Ed.), *Encyclopedia of positive psychology (Vol. 1)*, pp. 361–368. Oxford: Blackwell.
5. Martela, F., & Steger, M. (2016). The three meanings of meaning in life: Distinguishing coherence, purpose, and significance. *The Journal of Positive Psychology, 11*, 531–545.
6. George, L. S., & Park, C. L. (2017). The multidimensional existential meaning scale: A tripartite approach to measuring meaning in life. *The Journal of Positive Psychology, 12*, 613–627.
7. Twenge, J. M., Campbell, W. K., & Foster, C. A. (2003). Parenthood and marital satisfaction: A meta-analytic review. *Journal of Marriage and Family, 65*, 574–583.
8. Glass, J., Simon, R. W., & Andersson, M. A. (2016). Parenthood and happiness: Effects of work-family reconciliation policies in 22 OECD countries. *American Journal of Sociology, 122*, 886–929.
9. Nelson, S. K., Kushlev, K., & Lyubomirsky, S. (2014). The pains and pleasures of parenting: When, why, and how is parenthood associated with more or less well-being? *Psychological Bulletin, 140*, 846–895.
10. Baumeister, R. F., Vohs, K. D., Aaker, J., & Gabrinsky, E. N. (2013). Some key differences between a happy life and a meaningful life. *Journal of Positive Psychology, 8*, 505–516.
11. Abe, J. A. A. (2016). A longitudinal follow-up study of happiness and meaning-making. *The Journal of Positive Psychology, 11*, 489–498.
12. Vos, J. (2016). Working with meaning in life in mental health care: A systematic literature review of the practices and effectiveness of meaning-centered therapies. In P. Russo-Netzer et al. (Eds.), *Clinical perspectives on meaning* (pp. 59–87). Switzerland: Springer International Publishing.
13. Brietbart, W., Rosenfield, B., Pessin, H., Applebaum, A., Kulikowski, J., & Lichtenthal, W. G. (2015). Meaning-centered group psychotherapy: An effective intervention for improving psychological well-being in patients with advanced cancer. *Journal of Clinical Oncology, 33*, 749–754.

14. Canada, A. L., Murphy, P. E., Fitchett, G., & Stein, K. (2016). Re-examining the contributions of faith, meaning, and peace to quality of life: A report from the American Cancer Society's study of cancer survivors-II (SCS-II). *Annals of Behavioral Medicine, 50*, 79–86.

15. Roepke, A. M., Jayawickreme, E., & Riffle, O. M. (2014). Meaning and health: A systematic review. *Applied Research of Quality of Life, 9*, 1055–1079.

16. Yalom, I. (1980). *Existential psychotherapy*. New York, NY: Basic Books.

17. Koole, S., Greenberg, J., & Pyszczynski, T. (2006). Introducing science to the psychology of the soul: Experimental existential psychology. *Current Directions in Psychological Science, 15*, 212–216.

18. Taylor, S. E. (1983). Adjustment to threatening events: A theory of cognitive adaptations. *American Psychologist, 38*, 1161–1173.

19. Stillman, T. F., Baumeister, R. F., Lambert, N. M., Crescioni, A. W., DeWall, C. N., & Fincham, F. D. (2009). Alone and without purpose: Life loses meaning following social exclusion. *Journal of Experimental Social Psychology, 45*, 686–694.

20. Leary, M. R., Twenge, J. M., & Quinlivan, E. (2006). Interpersonal rejection as a determinant of anger and aggression. *Personality and Social Psychology Review, 10*, 111–132.

21. Erikson, E. H. (1950). *Childhood and society*. New York, NY: Norton.

22. Pyszczynski, T., Greenberg, J., Koole, S., & Solomon, S. (2010). Experimental existential psychology: Coping with the facts of life. In S. Fiske & D. Gilbert (Eds.), *Handbook of social psychology* (8th ed., 1, 724–757). New York, NY: Wiley.

23. Martin, L. L., Campbell, W. K., & Henry, C. D. (2004). The roar of awakening: Mortality acknowledgment as a call to authentic living. In J. Greenberg, S. Koole, & T. Pyszczynski (Eds.), *Handbook of experimental existential psychology* (pp. 431–448). New York, NY: Guilford Press.

24. Taylor, S. E. (1983). Adjustment to threatening events: A theory of cognitive adaptations. *American Psychologist, 38*, 1161–1173.

25. Hoorens, V. (1993). Self-enhancement and superiority biases in social comparison. *European Review of Social Psychology, 4*, 113–139.

26. Campbell, W. K., & Sedikides, C. (1999). Self-threat magnifies the self-serving bias: A meta-analytic integration. *Review of General Psychology, 3*, 23–43.

27. Lord, C. G., Ross, L., & Lepper, M. R. (1979). Biased assimilation and attitude polarization: The effects of prior theories on subsequently considered evidence. *Journal of Personality and Social Psychology, 37*, 2098–2109.

28. Dweck, C. S. (2006). *Mindset: The new psychology of success*. New York, NY: Penguin Random House.

29. Van Tongeren, D. R., & Burnette, J. L. (2018). Do you believe happiness can change? Effects of happiness mindsets on well-being and satisfaction. *The Journal of Positive Psychology, 13*, 101–109.

30. Bowlby, J. (1969). *Attachment and loss.* New York, NY: Basic Books.
31. Hook, J. N., Davis, D. E., Owen, J., Worthington, E. L., & Utsey, S. O. (2013). Cultural humility: Measuring openness to culturally diverse clients. *Journal of Counseling Psychology, 60,* 353–366.
32. Brown, C. B. (2012). *Daring greatly: How the courage to be vulnerable transforms the way we live, love, parent, and lead.* New York, NY: Gotham.
33. Hayes, S. C., Wilson, K. G., Gifford, E. V., Follette, V. M., & Strosahl, K. (1996). Experiential avoidance and behavioral disorders: A functional dimensional approach to diagnosis and treatment. *Journal of Clinical and Consulting Psychology, 64,* 1152–1168.
34. Machell, K. A., Goodman, F. R., & Kashdan, T. B. (2015). Experiential avoidance and well-being: A daily diary analysis. *Cognition and Emotion, 29,* 351–359.
35. Ruiz, F. J. (2010). A review of acceptance and commitment therapy (ACT) empirical evidence: Correlational, experimental psychopathology, component and outcome studies. *International Journal of Psychology & Psychological Therapy, 10,* 125–162.
36. Chawla, N., & Ostafin, B. (2007). Experiential avoidance as a functional dimensional approach to psychopathology: An empirical review. *Journal of Clinical Psychology, 63,* 871–890.
37. Muraven, M., & Baumeister, R. F. (2000). Self-regulation and depletion of limited resources: Does self-control resemble a muscle? *Psychological Bulletin, 126,* 247–259.
38. Van Tongeren, D. R., DeWall, C. N., Green, J. D., Cairo, A. H., Davis, D. E., & Hook, J. N. (2018). Self-regulation facilitates meaning in life. *Review of General Psychology, 22,* 95–106.
39. Brown, K. W., & Ryan, R. M. (2003). The benefits of being present: Mindfulness and its role in psychological well-being. *Journal of Personality and Social Psychology, 84*(4), 822.
40. Trails to Wellness. (n.d.). *Physical coping: Knowing the difference.* Online resource. Accessed at https://storage.trailstowellness.org/resources/mindfulness/knowing-the-difference-when-to-use-mindfulness-distress-tolerance-and-other-tools-mindfulness.pdf
41. Burns, D. D. (1981). *Feeling good: The new mood therapy.* New York, NY: Penguin Books.
42. Linehan, M. M. (1993). *Diagnosis and treatment of mental disorders. Cognitive-behavioral treatment of borderline personality disorder.* New York, NY: Guilford Press.
43. Rohr, R. (2011). *Falling upward: A spirituality for the two halves of life.* San Francisco, CA: Jossey-Bass.
44. Park, C. L. (2010). Making sense of the meaning literature: An integrative review of meaning making and its effects on adjustment to stressful life events. *Psychological Bulletin, 136,* 257–301.

45. Ross, L., Lepper, M. R., & Hubbard, M. (1975). Perseverance in self-perception and social perception: Biased attributional processes in the debriefing paradigm. *Journal of Personality and Social Psychology, 32,* 880–892.

46. Silver, R. C., & Updegraff, J. A. (2013). Searching for and finding meaning following personal and collective traumas. In K. D. Markman, T. Proulx, & M. J. Lindberg (Eds.), *The psychology of meaning* (pp. 237–255). Washington, DC: American Psychological Association.

47. Linley, P. A., & Joseph, S. (2004), Positive change following trauma and adversity: A review. *Journal of Traumatic Stress, 17,* 11–21.

48. Van Tongeren, D. R., Green, J. D., Davis, D. E.. Worthington, E. L., Jr., & Reid, C. A. (2013). Till death do us part: Terror management and forgiveness in close relationships. *Personal Relationships, 20,* 755–768.

49. Plusnin, N., Pepping, C., & Kashima, E. (2018). The role of close relationships in terror management: A systematic review and research agenda. *Personality and Social Psychology Review. 22,* 307–346.

50. Van Tongeren, D. R., Davis, D. E., Hook, J. N., & Johnson, K. A. (2016). Security versus growth: Existential tradeoffs of various religious perspectives. *Psychology of Religion and Spirituality, 8,* 77–88.

51. Baumeister, R. F. (1991). *Meanings in life.* New York, NY: Guilford Press.

52. White, M., & Epston, D. (1990). *Narrative means to therapeutic ends.* New York, NY: Norton.

53. Kelley, P. (1996). Narrative theory and social work treatment. In F. J. Turner (Ed.), *Social work treatment* (pp. 461–479). New York, NY: The Free Press.

54. Van Tongeren, D. R., DeWall, C. N., Chen, Z., Bulbilia, J., & Sibley, C. G. (2019). *Religious residue: Cross-cultural evidence that religious psychology and behavior persist following deidentification.* Manuscript submitted for publication.

55. Walsh, J. (2006). *Theories for direct social work practice.* Belmont, CA: Thomson.

56. Gungor, M., McHargue, M., McBride, E., & Matthews, W. (The Liturgists Podcast). (2019, March 7). *Fear|Live in Nashville* [Adapted from audio podcast]. Retrieved from http://www.theliturgists.com/podcast/2019/3/7/fear-live-in-nashville

57. Linley, P. A., & Joseph, S. (2011). Meaning in life and posttraumatic growth. *Journal of Loss and Trauma, 16,* 150–159.

58. Joseph, S., & Linley, P. A. (2005). Positive adjustment to threatening events: An organismic valuing theory of growth through adversity. *Review of General Psychology, 9,* 262–280.

59. McFarland, C., & Alvaro, C. (2000). The impact of motivation on temporal comparisons: Coping with traumatic events by perceiving personal growth. *Journal of Personality and Social Psychology, 79,* 327–343.

60. Jayawickreme, E., & Blackie, L. E. R. (2014). Posttraumatic growth as positive

personality change: Evidence, controversies and future directions. *European Journal of Personality, 28,* 312–331.

61. Frazier, P., Tennen, H., Gavian, M., Park, C., Tomich, P., & Tashiro, T. (2009). Does self-reported posttraumatic growth reflect genuine positive change? *Psychological Science, 20,* 912–919.

62. Jayawickreme, E., & Blackie, L. E. R. (2016). *Exploring the psychological benefits of hardship: A critical reassessment of posttraumatic growth.* Switzerland: Springer.

63. Kernis, M. H., & Goldman, B. M. (2006). A multicomponent conceptualization of authenticity: Theory and research. *Advances in Experimental Social Psychology, 38,* 283–357.

64. Ong, A. D., Bergeman, C. S., Bisconti, T. L., & Wallace, K. A. (2006). Psychological resilience, positive emotions, and successful adaptation to stress in later life. *Journal of Personality and Social Psychology, 91,* 730–749.

65. Windle, G. (2011). What is resilience? A review and concept analysis. *Review in Clinical Gerontology, 21,* 152–169.

66. Richardson, G. E. (2002). The metatheory of resilience and resiliency. *Journal of Clinical Psychology, 58,* 307–321.

67. Hart, J. (2014). Toward an integrative theory of psychological defense. *Perspectives on Psychological Science, 9,* 19–39.

68. Pyszczynski, T., Solomon, S., & Greenberg, J. (2015). Thirty years of terror management theory: From genesis to revelation. *Advances in Experimental Social Psychology, 52,* 1–70.

69. Van Tongeren, D. R., Davis, D. E., Hook, J. N., & Johnson, K. A. (2016). Security versus growth: Existential tradeoffs of various religious perspectives. *Psychology of Religion and Spirituality, 8,* 77–88.

70. Martin, L. L., Campbell, W. K., & Henry, C. D. (2004). The roar of awakening: Mortality acknowledgment as a call to authentic living. In J. Greenberg, S. Koole, & T. Pyszczynski (Eds.), *Handbook of experimental existential psychology* (pp. 431–448). New York, NY: Guilford Press.

71. Vail, K. E., Juhl, J., Arndt, J., Vess, M. K., Routledge, C., & Rutjens, B. T. (2012). When death is good for life: Considering the positive trajectories of terror management. *Personality and Social Psychology Review, 16,* 303–329.

72. Brown, C. B. (2012). *Daring greatly: How the courage to be vulnerable transforms the way we live, love, parent, and lead.* New York, NY: Gotham.

73. Routledge, C. (2018). *Meaning in modern America.* Institute for Family Studies Research Brief. https://ifstudies.org/ifs-admin/resources/ifsresearch brief-clayroutledgefindingmeaning.pdf

74. Stauner, N., Exline, J. J., Pargament, K. I., Wilt, J. A., & Grubbs, J. B. (2019). Stressful life events and religiousness predicts struggles about religion and spirituality. *Psychology of Religion and Spirituality, 11,* 291-296.

75. Park, C. (2005). Religion as a meaning-making framework in coping with life stress. *Journal of Social Issues, 61*, 707–729.

76. Lewis Hall, M. E., Shannonhouse, L., Aten, J., McMartin, J., & Silverman, E. J. (2018). Religion-specific resources for meaning-making from suffering: Defining the territory. *Mental Health, Religion, and Culture, 21*, 77-92.

77. Heine, S. J., Proulx, T., & Voh, K. D. (2006). The meaning maintenance model: On the coherence of social motivations. *Personality and Social Psychology Review, 10*, 88–110.

78. Van Tongeren, D. R., DeWall, C. N., Chen, Z., Bulbulia, J., & Sibley, C. (2019). *Cross-cultural evidence that religious psychology and behavior persist following deidentification.* Manuscript submitted for publication.

79. Stillman, T., Baumeister, R., Lambert, N., Crescioni, W., DeWall, C. N., & Fincham, F. (2009). Alone and without purpose: Life loses meaning following social exclusion. *Journal of Experimental Social Psychology, 45*, 686–694.

80. Pinel, E. C., Bernecker, S. L., & Rampy, N. M. (2015). I-sharing on the couch. On the clinical implications of shared subjective experiences. *Journal of Psychotherapy Integrations, 25*, 59–70.

81. Pennebaker, J. W. (1990). *Opening up: The healing powers of confiding in others.* New York, NY: William Morrow.

82. Haidt, J., & Kesebir, S. (2010). Morality. In S. Fiske, D. Gilbert, & G. Lindzey (Eds.), *The handbook of social psychology* (5th ed., pp. 797–832). Hoboken, NJ: Wiley.

83. Van Tongeren, D. R., Green, J. D., Davis, D. E., Hook, J. N., & Hulsey, T. L. (2016). Prosociality enhances meaning in life. *The Journal of Positive Psychology, 11*, 225–236.

84. Klein, N. (2017). Prosocial behavior increases perceptions of meaning in life. *The Journal of Positive Psychology, 12*, 354–361.

85. Gray, K., & Wegner, D. M. (2009). Moral typecasting: Divergent perceptions of moral agents and moral patients. *Journal of Personality and Social Psychology, 96*, 505–520.

86. Van Tongeren, D. R., Green, J. D., Hook, J. N., Davis, D. E., Davis, J. L., & Ramos, M. (2015). Forgiveness increases meaning in life. *Social Psychological and Personality Science, 6*, 47–55.

87. Van Tongeren, D. R., Hook, J. N., Ramos, M. J., Edwards, M., Worthington, E. L., Jr., Davis, D. E., ... Osae-Larbi, J. A. (2019). The complementarity of humility hypothesis: Individual, relational, and physiological effects of mutually humble partners. *The Journal of Positive Psychology, 14*(2), 178–187.

88. Van Tongeren, D. R., Davis, D. E., & Hook, J. N. (2014). Social benefits of humility: Initiating and maintaining romantic relationships. *The Journal of Positive Psychology, 9*, 313–321.

89. Farrell, J. E., Hook, J. N., Ramos, M., Davis, D. E., Van Tongeren, D. R., & Ruiz,

J. M. (2015). Humility and relationship outcomes in couples: The mediating role of commitment. *Couple and Family Psychology, 4,* 14–26.

90. Steger, M. F., Frazier, P., Oishi, S., & Kaler, M. (2006). The Meaning in Life Questionnaire: Assessing the presence of and search for meaning in life. *Journal of Counseling Psychology, 53,* 80–93.

91. Frazier, P., Greer, C., Gabrielsen, S., Tennen, H., Park, C., & Tomich, P. (2013). The relation between trauma exposure and prosocial behavior. *Psychological Trauma: Research, Practice, and Policy, 5,* 286–294.

92. Davis, D. E., Hook, J. N., Worthington, E. L., Jr., Van Tongeren, D. R., Gartner, A. L., Jennings, D. J. II, & Emmons, R. A. (2011). Relational humility: Conceptualizing and measuring humility as a personality judgment. *Journal of Personality Assessment, 93,* 225–234.

93. McElroy, S., Rice, K., Davis, D. E., Hook, J. N., Hill, P. C., Worthington E. L., Jr., & Van Tongeren, D. R. (2014). Intellectual humility and religious leadership. *Journal of Psychology and Theology, 42,* 19–30.

94. Lavelock, C. R., Worthington, E. L., Jr., Davis, D. E., Griffin, B. J., Reid, C. A., Hook, J. N., & Van Tongeren, D. R. (2014). The quiet virtue speaks: An intervention to promote humility. *Journal of Psychology and Theology, 42,* 99–110.

95. Worthington, E. L., Jr. (2006). *Forgiveness and reconciliation: Theory and application.* New York, NY: Routledge.

96. McCullough, M. E., Worthington, E. L., Jr., & Rachal, K. C. (1997). Interpersonal forgiveness in close relationships. *Journal of Personality and Social Psychology, 75,* 321–326.

97. Burnette, J. L., McCullough, M. E., Van Tongeren, D. R., & Davis, D. E. (2012). Forgiveness results from integrating information about relationship value and exploitation risk. *Personality and Social Psychology Bulletin, 38,* 345–356.

98. Worthington, E. L., Jr. (2006). *Forgiveness and reconciliation: Theory and application.* New York, NY: Routledge.

99. McCullough, M. E., Kilpatrick, S. D., Emmons, R. A., & Larson, D. B. (2001). Is gratitude a moral affect? *Psychological Bulletin, 127,* 249–266.

100. Wood, A. M., Froh, J. J., & Geraghty, A. W. A. (2010). Gratitude and well-being: A review and theoretical integration. *Clinical Psychology Review, 30,* 890–905.

101. Schnitker, S. A. (2012). An examination of patience and well-being. *The Journal of Positive Psychology, 7,* 263–280.

102. Schnitker, S. A., Houltberg, B., Dyrness, W., & Redmond, N. (2017). The virtue of patience, spirituality, and suffering: Integrating lessons from positive psychology, psychology of religion, and Christian theology. *Psychology of Religion and Spirituality, 9,* 264–275.

103. Snyder, C. R. (2002). Hope theory: Rainbows in the mind. *Psychological Inquiry, 13,* 249–275.

104. Root Luna, L. M., Van Tongeren, D. R., & Witvliet, C. V. O. (2017). Virtue,

positive psychology, and religion: Consideration of an overarching virtue and an underpinning mechanism. *Psychology of Religion and Spirituality, 9,* 299–302.

105. Carver, C. S., & Scheier, M. F. (2002). Control processes and self-organization as complementary principles underlying behavior. *Personality and Social Psychology Review, 6,* 304–315.

106. Baumeister, R. F., Vohs, K. D., & Tice, D. M. (2007). The strength model of self-control. *Current Directions in Psychological Science, 16*(6), 351–355.

Index

About the Authors

 **Daryl R. Van Tongeren, PhD,** is an associate professor of psychology at Hope College in Holland, Michigan. Daryl is a social psychologist and has published over 150 scholarly articles and chapters on topics such as meaning in life, religion, virtues (including forgiveness and humility), relationships, and well-being. His research has been supported by numerous grants from the John Templeton Foundation to explore topics including meaning in life, religion and religious de-identification, and humility, and his research has won national and international awards. He received a 2016 Rising Star designation from the Association for Psychological Science (APS), and he was named a Fellow of the International Society for Science and Religion (ISSR) and a Fellow of the Midwestern Psychological Association (MPA). Currently, he is an associate editor for *The Journal of Positive Psychology*, and a consulting editor for *Psychology of Religion and Spirituality* and *The Journal of Social Psychology*.

 **Sara A. Showalter Van Tongeren, LCSW,** is a licensed clinical social worker in the states of Michigan and Virginia and is a graduate of the Virginia Commonwealth University School of Social Work in Richmond, Virginia. Sara has more than twelve years of clinical social work experience in settings such as private practice, foster care, inpatient hospitals and outpatient

medical clinics, interpartner violence shelters, and behavioral health. She is a member of the National Association of Social Workers (NASW). Currently, she owns a private practice in Holland, Michigan, where she works with individuals, couples, families, and children to help them cultivate a sense of meaning and develop narratives of resilience following trauma and unexpected life events. Sara specializes in cognitive-behavioral therapy, mindfulness, existential psychotherapy, narrative therapy, brainspotting, and acceptance commitment therapy.